HIA
KAI

GODWIT

UK | USA | Canada | Ireland | Australia
India | New Zealand | South Africa | China

Godwit is an imprint of the Penguin Random House group of companies,
whose addresses can be found at global.penguinrandomhouse.com.

First published by Penguin Random House New Zealand, 2020

9 10 8

Text © Monique Fiso, 2020

Photography © Manja Wachsmuth, 2020: back cover (left), 2–3, 6, 8, 11, 12–13, 18, 22, 25, 26, 31, 32, 33, 38, 44,
45, 50, 51, 52, 54, 55, 57, 58, 60, 61, 64, 65–6, 70 (top right, bottom left and right), 72, 75, 76, 78, 82 (left), 84
(top right, bottom left and right), 86, 89, 93, 94, 98 (top left and right, bottom left), 101, 102, 106, 107, 109, 112,
116, 120, 123, 124, 126 (top left), 129, 130 (top right, bottom left), 134, 136, 138, 141, 142-3, 149, 159, 167, 173, 195,
209, 240, 245, 251, 264–5.
Photography © Amber-Jayne Bain, 2020: back cover (centre and right), 70 (top left), 81, 82 (right), 84 (top
left), 90, 96, 98 (bottom right), 119, 126 (top right, bottom left and right), 130 (top left, bottom right), 147, 151,
153, 155, 157, 161, 163, 165, 169, 171, 175, 179, 181, 183, 185, 187, 189, 191, 193, 197, 199, 201, 203, 205, 206, 210, 212,
215, 217, 219, 220, 223, 225, 226, 229, 231, 233, 235, 237, 239, 243, 247, 248, 253, 255, 257, 258, 261.

The moral right of the author has been asserted.

Cover and internal design by Cat Taylor © Penguin Random House New Zealand
Initial cover concepts by Rachel Clark © Penguin Random House New Zealand
Front cover photograph by Manja Wachsmuth
Prepress by Image Centre Group
Printed and bound in China by RR Donnelley

The information contained in this book is of a general nature only – and foraging for ingredients should be
treated with caution. If you do wish to make use of any information in this book, you should first consider the
appropriateness and safety to do so, including the possible need to consult an expert.

A catalogue record for this book is available from the National Library of New Zealand.

ISBN 978-0-14-377260-6

Monique Fiso

WITH LUCY CORRY AND TRACY BERNO
PHOTOGRAPHY BY MANJA WACHSMUTH AND AMBER-JAYNE BAIN

HIA KAI

MODERN MĀORI CUISINE

GODWIT

CONTENTS

MY STORY

When I returned home after seven years in New York, I was unsure of what I wanted to do next. I was 28 years old and I had accomplished so much, but I was burnt out from the hard mahi (work) that comes with working in one of the most competitive cities in the culinary world. I also missed my family, and I wanted to see the next generation of my whānau grow.

Being far from Aotearoa had made me realise there was a disconnect. I had studied and mastered many different cuisines and cooking techniques but I knew very little about the food of my own whakapapa (genealogy). I didn't grow up knowing a lot about my Māori heritage; as I got older I wanted to connect with it and realised I could do this through food.

As a chef, I want my food to challenge people and their assumptions – it has to be delicious and creative but it also has to tell a story. I started to discuss Māori cuisine with people and the general feedback centred around hāngi, fry bread and boil-up. I knew this couldn't be the whole story and didn't represent people whose ancestors were so deeply connected to the land and the natural environment. I didn't

realise at the time that the story I would begin to tell would be my own.

When I was a kid, I was a fussy eater but I was always fascinated with food. Growing up, in Porirua, Wellington, I realised from an early age that different people ate different things. My dad is Sāmoan and my mum is half-Māori, half-Pākehā. My Māori grandfather, Richard Hurunui, passed away before I was born, but when we went to my grandma's house for Sunday lunch we'd eat things like pea and ham soup or roast lamb with potatoes. Then, when we went to my Sāmoan Nan's house, we'd have chop suey, corn beef, taro and lūʻau. It was all delicious to me, especially because my parents were working long hours while also studying and raising five children, so they didn't have much time to cook.

From a young age, I would help Nan prepare Sunday lunch. I loved it – the other kids would be outside playing but I'd be standing on a chair cutting the vermicelli noodles for chop suey. By the time I was 17, I knew I wanted to be a chef. I left school and enrolled in WelTec's cookery and patisserie diplomas. My parents weren't happy about me leaving school. I had next to no money but I knew I had to make it work. To build up my experience, I worked in as many kitchens as I could fit in around my class schedule and homework.

Midway through the course, I needed to complete 50 hours' work experience, and I secured a placement at Martin Bosley's, one of Aotearoa's leading and award-winning restaurants at the time. I did the 50 hours in my first week, and then just kept showing up and working for free until I was offered a job. I learned so much from Martin; he was the first chef to open my eyes to how food and art can be intertwined on a plate. In many ways, Martin's food was ahead of its time in pre-foodie culture Aotearoa, but that never stopped him from pushing the boundaries and daring diners to try things they'd never encountered before on a menu.

After a couple of years working under Martin, I decided to go abroad in order to challenge myself. I sold everything I owned and bought a one-way ticket to New York. Within a few hours of landing, I hit the ground running in search of a job. I'd never been to New York, and this was before smartphones, so I spent most of the morning getting lost and asking strangers for directions. At some point in the early afternoon of day one, I found myself walking up the concrete steps of PUBLIC restaurant ready to try my luck. PUBLIC was nestled in the trendy neighbourhood of Nolita

and was known for serving an eclectic mix of Asian-meets-Antipodean cuisine. Executive Chef Brad Farmerie had spent many years working in London under celebrated Kiwi chef Peter Gordon at his renowned restaurant Providores. Perhaps it was his fondness of Kiwis, but whatever the reason, Brad put me on the sauté station and my time in New York kitchens officially began.

I had only planned to spend one year in New York, but I'd end up staying much, much longer. When I think of my time in New York, it feels like a blur. I was so focused on my craft I just put my head down and worked. Eighty-hour weeks were the norm, and days off were few and far between. It was hard, but it was worth it.

At the end of 2015, I was feeling the pull of home and I moved back with no concrete plans. A few friends suggested that I should open my own restaurant. The problem was, I couldn't imagine what a restaurant with me at the helm really looked like. New York had left me highly skilled, but the pace of the city and restaurant life hadn't afforded me time to think about the sort of dining experience I'd like to create. I took a seasonal job as a private chef at a lodge in Hanmer Springs. I went from working in the intensity of the Big Apple to living in a small town on the outskirts of North Canterbury but it gave me the time and space to collect my thoughts. By the end of that three months I'd evolved my style; my plates

now had their own distinct voice. I started developing the idea of celebrating Māori cuisine.

Taking this to Aotearoa's dining scene was always going to be a challenge. I was really scared. I ran the idea past Matt Lambert, of The Musket Room fame, who I'd worked with in New York, and he said, 'Just do it'. He put me in touch with Mike Meredith to see if I could use Merediths for a pop-up, and that was the push off the ledge that I needed. I thought no one would be interested and I'd consider it a success if I sold 20 tickets. I couldn't have been more wrong. There was so much demand that I spent the rest of the year holding a series of pop-ups around the country which all sold out. I was surprised and pleased that people were so enthusiastic, but it still didn't feel quite right. I knew I hadn't captured the cultural aspects that I wanted to celebrate; the food was good but it didn't tell a story.

That all changed when I met Joe McLeod in late 2016. We met for a cup of tea on Boxing Day, then a couple of days later he took me on a bush walk. Joe had wanted to do something similar in the 1980s, but there wasn't a huge appetite at the time. I ended up spending most of the next two months learning from Joe – he taught me about traditional uses of native plants and how to weave. Then he'd test me on my knowledge and we'd make hāngi together. At the end of my summer with Joe, I realised what I'd been missing.

I started with hāngi. I wanted to find out how far you could push that style of cooking to make it more contemporary. When many New Zealanders think about hāngi, they envisage steamed food cooked in tinfoil. That's light years away from a hāngi where food has been wrapped in harakeke, pukapuka and rangiora. When you do it the traditional way, the flavour profile is completely different.

In 2017, I took that knowledge and turned it into a series of outdoor pop-ups around the country. They were popular and more people started to get interested in what I was doing. The pop-ups were amazing, but I was getting frustrated. It's hard to build a team or do proper research and development when you're constantly on the move. I knew what I was doing had incredible potential, but it needed a permanent space. People loved the hāngi experience, but I wanted to focus more heavily on indigenous ingredients. I wanted to create a modern dining experience and a new chapter for the next generation of chefs.

In late 2018, we opened Hiakai in a historic building in the inner-city Wellington suburb of Mount Cook. A couple of months later, *TIME* magazine named the restaurant as one of its 'Greatest Places of 2019'.

As a chef, my style is avant-garde and influenced by the stories I want to tell. What I create has to have meaning. At Hiakai, we showcase an indigenous ingredient in every dish. A lot of people describe what we do as thought-provoking, even polarising at times. I would never change that about us.

Hiakai represents a new era for Māori cuisine. We believe that food and drink is more than a commodity, it's a medium for cultural exchange and change. We take inspiration from our home, Aotearoa.

HOW TO USE THIS BOOK + A NOTE ON FORAGING

It's my hope that this book will help you look at Māori cuisine in a new way, to understand and respect the rich history, culture and knowledge that it contains.

I've spent a long time learning about traditional Māori hunting, cultivation and cooking – and discovering how to weave all this information into practical ways of gathering and eating. It hasn't been easy – until now, there hasn't been one singular book that you could read to find out how to do all these things.

There has been a lot of trial and error, and my team and I have learned from every mistake. I want to share what I've learned in the hope that the next generation of chefs build on what we've discovered so far. You might never have considered eating some of the indigenous ingredients featured in this book, or even known they were edible. Or you may have specific taste memories linked to bitter pūhā or sweet kūmara – and be pleasantly surprised to

find that they can be used in contemporary dishes as well as traditional ones. Some of the recipes require equipment or skills not often found in domestic kitchens, but others are more achievable for home cooks. Either way, I hope the recipes will stimulate your curiosity and creativity.

I also hope that you'll be motivated to look more closely at ngā tipu (indigenous plants) around you when you're next exploring our lush ngahere (forest). We're lucky to live in such a bountiful and productive landscape, where indigenous plants are found everywhere from small city reserves to vast national parks. If you're going to go foraging though, keep some basic protocols in mind. Don't forage in areas that may be polluted or toxic, such as roadside verges that absorb vehicle emissions or that may have been sprayed. Don't taste or eat anything you can't identify or you're not sure about. Follow the rules and regulations for foraging in a certain area, whether that's getting permission from the landowner or obtaining a licence. Only pick or harvest what you need – take a third, leave a third for next time and leave a third to regenerate.

Hiakai is the Māori word for hungry, or having a craving for food. I think it captures everything about what we are trying to do; to fill up our bellies and our minds with the indigenous ingredients that nourished our ancestors. I'm proud to be able to share this kai with you.

1—
THE BEGINNING

Ka mua, ka muri

*Walking backwards
into the future*

Every story is different. This is the way we tell our story, the story of our kai.

In the beginning, there was nothing.

The story begins in the void known as Te Kore. Te Kore is nothingness but it's also the beginning of everything. A place of unlimited potential.

After Te Kore came Te Pō. Te Pō was the time of darkness and the unknown, but also a time of becoming. What became in Te Pō was Ranginui and Papatūānuku. It's from them that all living things are descended.

In this place of no light, no sun, no moon, no stars, no wind, only darkness, Papatūānuku lay naked. Ranginui saw Papatūānuku and desired her, so he descended and took her as his wife. Ranginui and Papatūānuku lay in a loving embrace, so close that no light could get through. Papatūānuku bore her many sons into this dark world. Six of them – Tāne-mahuta, Tangaroa, Tāwhirimātea, Tūmatauenga, Haumia-tiketike and Rongo-mā-Tāne – lay cramped between their parents.

Ranginui and Papatūānuku held each other so tightly that their children could barely move. Trapped in the blackness, the sons plotted to let light into their world. All of them, except Tāwhirimātea, decided that separating their parents was the only way to gain freedom.

Tūmatauenga, the fiercest, believed killing their parents was the best way to split them. Tāne-mahuta disagreed. He thought their parents should be forced apart; Ranginui could ascend and become the sky father, while Papatūānuku could stay below and nurture them as the earth mother. Rongo-mā-Tāne agreed. He tried to push his parents apart with his hands but they wouldn't budge. Tangaroa, Haumia-tiketike and Tūmatauenga joined him, but they were unable to break their parents' loving bond. Finally, Tāne-mahuta, with his shoulders to the ground and his legs pushing upwards, prised Ranginui and Papatūānuku apart.

The couple cried out with surprise and grief but Tāne-mahuta ignored them, planting posts to keep them far from each other. To this day, when the rain falls from the sky and the mist rises from the land we are reminded of Ranginui and Papatūānuku's eternal grief. Tāne-mahuta became known as Tāne-te-toko-o-te-rangi – Tāne the prop of the heavens, the forests of Tāne being where the canopy of great tōtara and kauri reach skyward.

And so, Te Pō was over. The separation of Ranginui and Papatūānuku heralded the emergence of Te Ao Marama – the space between the heavens and the earth, the world of light and existence.

NGĀ ATUA AND KAI MĀORI: FOOD OF THE GODS

Tāwhirimātea was enraged that his brothers, especially Tāne, had severed their parents' union. He ascended to the sky to join his father and convinced a reluctant Ranginui to help him wage war. All the brothers, except Tūmatauenga, fled in fear of his wrath: Tāne into the dense forest, Tangaroa into the sea, Rongo-mā-Tāne and Haumia-tiketike into the earth.

Furious at Tāne, Tāwhirimātea destroyed his forests with winds that roared with great force. He next set his sights on his brother Tangaroa. He started huge storms that whipped up waves the size of mountains, causing Tangaroa's son Punga and his children Ikatere and Tū-te-wehiwehi to flee in different directions: Tū-te-wehiwehi went inland, where he became the father of all reptiles; Ikatere sought safety in the depths of the ocean, where his descendants include Pātiki (flounder), Kōkiri (leatherjacket), Whaitere (stingray), Wheketoro (octopus) and Tāmure (snapper).

Rongo-mā-Tāne and Haumia-tiketike escaped Tāwhirimātea's wrath by taking refuge deep in Papatūānuku's body; their loving mother hid them until the storm

had passed. Rongo-mā-Tāne became the protector of cultivated plants (including kūmara) and the guardian of agriculture; Haumia-tiketike became the atua (god) of wild, uncultivated plants, including aruhe, the edible fern root. These plants are still found in this underground home.

Tāwhirimātea's vengeance was incomplete, however. He had one remaining brother to fight: the defiant Tūmatauenga, who had wanted to kill Ranginui and Papatūānuku. The brothers were well matched, and Tāwhirimātea was unable to defeat his brother. He withdrew to the sky to be with Ranginui. Here he continues to reside, still sending down storms to provoke his brothers.

Victorious Tūmatauenga was angry that his brothers had left him alone to face Tāwhirimātea. He sought utu (vengeance). First, he attacked Tāne's children, making snares and spears from the trees and vines, so that his brother's descendants could no longer fly free. He made canoes, hooks and nets to catch Tangaroa's children. He dug holes in the ground to capture the children of Rongo-mā-Tāne and Haumia-tiketike, heaping the fern roots and kūmara into kete to be eaten.

Thanks to Tūmatauenga's actions, we can today harness the resources of the natural world. We can hunt and eat birds (the children of Tāne), take to the waters and catch fish (the children of Tangaroa), cultivate and harvest food from plants (the children of Rongo-mā-Tāne and Haumia-tiketike).

And so, the children of Ranginui and Papatūānuku became ngā atua kaitiaki – the guardians of everything in the natural world, the place from which all our kai comes. This is the whakapapa of our food.

KAITIAKITANGA

Our natural resources descend from the atua; there is an interconnected relationship between all things. The land, sea, rivers, plants and animals all have a mauri, a wairua – a life force, a spirit. The gifts of the land, sky and waters are taonga. Their physical and spiritual health is of immense importance to us all. By following tikanga and mātauranga – protocol and knowledge – kaitiakitanga watches over the health and sustainability of the natural resources that nurture, grow and support our kai.

Kaitiakitanga is about more than simple guardianship, however. It's an inherited and inherent obligation to fulfil spiritual, ancestral responsibilities that whakapapa back to Ranginui and Papatūānuku, the atua kaitiaki of all the natural world. Kaitiakitanga is the responsibility to maintain mana over our precious resources and, in doing so, ensure the well-being of the people the resources support.

Kaitiakitanga is reflected in respecting life cycles for planting, gathering and harvesting, the karakia that are offered and the observance of rāhui (a ritual prohibition set for a good period of time). Kaitiakitanga pays respect to and fulfils inherent obligations to the taonga, the atua and the tūpuna (ancestors), while also looking ahead to safeguard our resources for future generations.

KARAKIA MŌ TE KAI

Nau mai e ngā hua
o te wao
o te ngakīnga
o te wai tai
o te wai māori.
Nā Tāne
nā Rongo
nā Tangaroa
nā Maru.
Ko Ranginui e tū iho nei
ko Papatūānuku e takoto ake nei.
Tūturu whakamaua kia tina
tina, haumi ē, hui ē, taiki ē!

Welcome the gifts of food
from the sacred forests
from the cultivated gardens
from the sea
from the fresh waters.
The food of Tāne
of Rongo
of Tangaroa
of Maru.
I acknowledge Ranginui who is above me
Papatūānuku who lies beneath me.
Let this be my commitment to all
draw together, affirm!

MARAMATAKA: THE MĀORI LUNAR CALENDAR

Kaitiakitanga reflects the intimate relationship between people, the land and the environment. One way this is honoured is through maramataka, the Māori lunar calendar. Māori have long looked to the moon for guidance on many community activities and to signal whether the coming season will be a bountiful one.

The Māori calendar commences in June, when the Matariki star cluster reappears. This marks the start of the New Year – a time of new beginnings and festivities that celebrate the continuity of past and present. Maramataka guides seasonal and daily kai-related activities. It identifies appropriate and inappropriate times for food gathering – planting and harvesting of crops, foraging and hunting, and the catching and collecting of kaimoana. As with other aspects of the natural environment, there is a link between the environment, the moon, the stars and the atua. The rhythms of the moon and constellations influence the waters of the ocean by causing tides, as well as bringing nourishment to the soil and enhancing the wairua of the kai grown in it. The fishing, planting and harvesting activities associated with the different seasons and days of the calendar are tikanga built by iwi, in different regions and over generations.

The lunar year is divided into four seasons (although there are differences between iwi): raumati (summer), ngahuru (autumn), kōanga (spring) and takurua (winter). Each of the seasons corresponds with a series of activities to do with procuring food depending on where one lives, the local climate and the availability of edible plants, birds and seafood.

There are 12 months in the Māori calendar year:

HONGONUI (OR HŌNGONGOI, JUNE–JULY)

Kua tino mātao te tangata, me te tahutahu ahi, ka pāinaina.
Man is now extremely cold and kindles fires before which he basks.

HERETURIKŌKĀ (JULY–AUGUST)

Kua kitea te kainga a te ahi i ngā turi o te tangata.
The scorching effect of fire is seen on the knees of man.

MAHURU (AUGUST–SEPTEMBER)
Kua pūmahana te whenua, me ngā otaota, me ngā rākau.
The earth has now acquired warmth, as have vegetation and trees.

WHIRINGA-Ā-NUKU (SEPTEMBER–OCTOBER)
Kua tino mahana te whenua.
The earth has now become quite warm.

WHIRINGA-Ā-RANGI (OCTOBER–NOVEMBER)
Kua raumati, kua kaha te rā.
It has now become summer and the sun is stronger.

HAKIHEA (NOVEMBER–DECEMBER)
Kua noho ngā manu kai roto i te kōhanga.
Birds are now sitting on their nests.

KOHITĀTEA (DECEMBER–JANUARY)
Kua makuru te kai: ka kai te tangata i ngā kai hou o te tau.
Fruits are now ripe and man eats the new food of the season.

HUITANGURU (JANUARY–FEBRUARY)
Kua tau te waewae o Ruhi kai whenua.
The foot of Ruhi (a summer star) now rests upon the earth.

POUTŪTERANGI (FEBRUARY–MARCH)
Kua hauhake te kai.
The crops are now harvested.

PAENGAWHĀWHĀ (MARCH–APRIL)
Kua putu ngā tupu o ngā kai i ngā paenga o ngā māra.
All the stalks of the plants are now stacked at the borders of the plantations.

HARATUA (APRIL–MAY)
Kua uru ngā kai kai te rua, kua mutu ngā mahi a te tangata.
Crops are now stored in pits. The tasks of man are finished.

PIPIRI (MAY–JUNE)
Ka pipiri ngā mea katoa i te whenua i te mātao, me te tangata.
All things on earth are contracted because of the cold; likewise, man.

Each new month begins on the night of the new moon, and each night of the month has its own name. Whiro is the first night of the new moon; Mutuwhenua is the last. Each night and phase of the moon is associated with food-gathering activities: some are favourable, others less so; some are even unlucky.

MAHINGA KAI: THE GATHERING PLACES

Mahinga kai can be understood to mean many different things. It concerns the resources of the land, forest, foreshore and sea from where we take our food. It refers to both our food-gathering places and the food gathered there, but it also has a much deeper reach. Mahinga kai has its roots in tikanga and is rich in mātauranga Māori. When Ranginui and Papatūānuku were forced apart, Te Ao Marama heralded the emergence of the natural world – the world from which all our kai comes. When we eat these foods, we are expressing this whakapapa and affirming our relationship with the land and our ancestors. Mahinga kai is the natural connection between the atua, the land, the people and their food. Every time food is gathered, whether from the garden, forest or water, the balance of the mauri of the resources must be protected, now and for future generations. These relationships are honoured through our customs and practices – the way in which we plant, harvest, gather and hunt our kai.

Food of the land

FRUITS OF THE FOREST

When the first Māori arrived in Aotearoa, they found a verdant land rich in kaimoana, birds and forageable fruits and berries. While this new land lacked the familiar plants of their previous tropical home, these early explorers had brought seeding crops to plant in their new environment. Unfortunately, only six crops were hardy enough to survive in New Zealand's temperate climate: kūmara, hue (gourd), aute (paper mulberry), taro, uwhi (yam) and tī pore (Pacific cabbage tree).

Māori developed sophisticated agricultural techniques that helped them produce these and other food crops. But, with only one harvest a year, they relied on hunting and foraging to stay fed. Over time, they developed a vast knowledge of the land and the food that could be harvested from it.

Māori had names for more than 50 types of soil, over 100 birds, 60 types of earthworm and more than 300 plants. There are estimated to be at least 190

AT HOME PARIHAKA WOMAN SCRAPING POTATOES WITH A SHELL 441

edible native plants in Aotearoa, and Māori used most of them; their roots, leaves, berries and even the trunks of trees all provided kai.

Aruhe, the underground roots of the widely found rārahu (bracken fern), became the most important wild vegetable. There are many stories about its origins. Some believe aruhe was the grandchild of Rarotimu and Rorotake, and grew on Ranginui's back. When Ranginui and Papatūānuku were separated, aruhe fell to the ground. Others believe the fern-root fronds are the hair of Haumia-tiketike, sticking up through the ground after he took refuge from the wrath of Tāwhirimātea in the body of Papatūānuku. Others believe that aruhe came on a waka from Hawaiki, or that the root

came from the fairy-like beings tūrehu or patupaiarehe. Aruhe was harvested throughout the year, though late spring to early summer was considered best. Each community had its own prized places to dig aruhe and much effort went into conserving them.

Harvesting was backbreaking. The rhizomes near the surface were stringy and hard; the best roots were usually found 50 centimetres deep. Traditionally, these roots, which could measure 30 centimetres long and more than 7 centimetres in diameter, were dug up by men using pointed sticks. These digging sticks, or kō, could be up to 3.5 metres long and were usually made from hardwood such as mānuka. They had a moveable footrest-style step near the pointed end, lashed to

Group outside a cookhouse in Parihaka, circa 1900.
Ref: 1/1-012053-G. Alexander Turnbull Library,
Wellington, New Zealand.

the kō with tough stems of a climbing vine called aka. Some kō were adorned with a crescent-shaped end, showing the moon's importance to the planting and gathering of kai.

After the soil was turned over by repeated digging, a wauwau (paddle-shaped spade) was sometimes used. Diggers recited a karakia to ensure a plentiful harvest.

Once the aruhe had been harvested, women carried vast bundles of roots back to the village and stacked them in short lengths to dry in the sun and wind, before they were packed in kete or hung in bundles from a storehouse roof. Prepared like this, they lasted almost indefinitely.

Aotearoa's forests were a rich source of kai. Kōrito (young leaf shoots) and a mealy substance from the tap roots and stems of the fast-growing, self-propagating tī (cabbage trees) were regularly eaten. Certain varieties, like tī pore and tī para, were better than others and were eventually cultivated in select areas. Tī kōuka was a particularly important source of food on the South Island's east coast, where kūmara was hard to cultivate. Its roots and stems were harvested in the spring. The stems were cut about a foot above the ground so the tree could rejuvenate. Each of the hewn logs (about 1.2 metres long) was split in two vertically, cleaned and left to dry for a month before being packed into large kete made of tī leaves. These kete, which

could hold upwards of 50 trunks, were steamed in a giant hāngi, then dried again. The resulting kāuru (the food produced from tī kōuka) was then taken to a pātaka (elevated storehouse) for long-term storage. Kāuru was such an important source of food for Ngāi Tahu that the place of the giant hāngi was named 'Te Umu Kaha', now known as Temuka.

Many forest foods were sought after but not eaten regularly. The hearts and berries of the abundant nīkau palm were much enjoyed but harvesting the edible heart meant killing the entire tree. The slow-growing mamaku (large black tree fern) was another occasional indulgence. The frond stems and the trunk contain a sago-like substance, but the fern doesn't regenerate when felled, and it was protected by various tapu.

Many important forest foods, like pikopiko (the koru or new shoots of the mamaku), were found at ground level. Pikopiko were gathered and eaten in the spring and summer, but harvesting them was a complex process. The koru are slimy when first cut; the outer layers of the trunk were stripped with stone adzes so that the slime could drain away. Alternatively, the koru could be cut and hung to dry.

Some forest food sources, like raupō and pūhā, were available year round. In swampy marshlands throughout Aotearoa, the sweet pollen of the raupō (bulrush) was collected in bark vessels and made into cakes called pungapunga. Gathering raupō took precision and patience. The flowerheads were picked before dawn and late in the evening, then spread on mats and left to dry in the sun during the day. Once dry, the flowers were stripped from the stems and sifted through baskets of finely woven flax by the principal male in each family. After this lengthy process, the pollen could be baked into cakes, which some Pākehā described as tasting like gingerbread. The roots were harvested in times of scarcity, to be eaten immediately or dried and stored.

The tender young leaves and buds of pūhā were gathered daily (sometimes twice a day) and eaten both raw and cooked. No part of this vital green vegetable was wasted; even the cooking juices were drunk.

Less commonly used green vegetables were kōkihi (beach spinach) and hānea (cress). Kōkihi occupies a unique position in Māori lore. Although initially a foraged plant, kōkihi was also cultivated, and so belongs to the realm of Rongo-mā-Tāne. However, thanks to its coastal growing environment, kōhihi's spiritual relationship extends to Tangaroa as well.

Fungi (harore – mushrooms; hakeke – wood-ear fungus) was also collected from the forest, found growing on dead timber. An abundance of fungi was a bad sign that a lean year was coming.

Other foraged foods included ngā hua ngahere: the fruits of the forest's various trees, shrubs and vines. These were a vital source of nutrients but many were tricky to harvest, requiring specialised preparation to make them palatable or non-toxic to eat. The fruits of the kahikatea, rimu, matAī and tōtara had to be picked from towering trees that were risky to climb. To reach the highly valued berries of the hīnau tree, for example, Māori had to climb 12–18 metres to the tree's canopy, using a ladder lashed to the trunk. The climbers would suspend a basket between two branches to collect the crop, then lower full baskets to the ground by cords. Empty baskets would be hauled back up the tree to minimise climbing and allow sizeable amounts to be picked in one session.

CULTIVATING THE LAND

Māori were skilled horticulturists long before they reached Aotearoa. The plants they grew successfully in their new home shaped their culture and society.

All food was valued but the kūmara was the paramount cultivated crop. Its whakapapa traces back to the battle that raged after Ranginui and Papatūānuku were forced apart. Rongo-mā-Tāne fled and took refuge in the body of his mother Papatūānuku, where he became the guardian of agriculture and protector of cultivated plants, including kūmara. The goddess Pani-tinaku, whom some describe as Rongo-mā-Tāne's daughter, gave birth to the kūmara after being impregnated with seeds that her husband Rongonui

stole from his older brother Whānui.

Because the original kūmara came from the heavens it had tapu origins. When Pani gave birth to it, Rongonui asked her to prepare te umu tapu (a sacred oven) to cook it, so that the tapu could be lifted. With this, kūmara became a taonga, the sacred food that sustained Māori life.

Everything connected to the kūmara, from planting through to harvesting, cooking and consumption, was sacred and involved particular rituals. Serious work went into preparing planting grounds. Māori used a slash-and-burn and rotation method for most agriculture, including kūmara cultivation. This was a crucial way to prepare the ground and enrich the soil. (Māori didn't use animal manure.) An area would be cultivated for two or three years, then burned to clear the land. The ground would be left to lie fallow for several years before being replanted, often allowing aruhe to grow in the interim.

Kūmara thrives in light and porous, sandy or gravelly soil, which warms up quickly and retains heat. When land was cleared, any remaining ash was dug in, often with the addition of more ash and baskets of sand and gravel to aerate the soil and improve drainage. The black charcoal and ash also absorbed sunlight, so the soil became warmer.

The call of the pīpīwharauroa (shining cuckoo) singing 'Koia, koia!' ('Dig, dig!') and the kōwhai's buds opening into bright yellow blossoms heralded the season for preparing kūmara grounds. Cultivating kūmara was a communal undertaking.

When the people gathered at the māra (garden), a karakia was given, asking the atua to bless their labour. Men worked at the front, using kō to loosen the soil and remove any stumps or rocks. Women and children followed behind, using club-shaped patupatu and timo (small hand-held grubbers) to break up clods. Timo were often made from a forked branch, with a flattened blade and a round handle, and could be used in a squatting position to break up the soil.

Before the main crop was planted, a ceremonial kūmara planting (māra tautāne) took place a distance away from the main gardens. These tubers were set aside for the atua. When the main crop was planted, special karakia were given and an offering (usually a bird) was made

to the gods. The tohunga (chosen expert) would put a tapu in place to protect the plantation and keep people away from it until harvest time.

Kūmara gardens were well known for their tidiness. The plants were grown in tupuke (mounds), approximately 60 centimetres apart, arranged in neat rows running from east to west. Light fences or stands of mānuka shielded them from destructive winds. Strict protocols, influenced by the maramataka, governed planting. At the optimum time, each tipu (seed kūmara) was placed in a mound facing the warmer north or sometimes the north-east. This was the direction of both the rising sun and the mythical land of Hawaiki, which was believed to be the source of fertility and the origin of kūmara. Planting was accompanied by more karakia.

The mauri of the crops was protected by stone carvings (taumata atua) in the image of Rongo-mā-Tāne, or by atua kiato (wooden pegs with carved heads) inserted into the ground and sometimes topped with skulls or preserved heads.

Endless work, usually performed by skilled and experienced kuia, went into keeping plantations free of weeds and predators. The surrounding earth was tilled and heaped up, and dead leaves trimmed. Weeds were removed with a ketu, a small paddle-like tool used to loosen the soil around the kūmara plants.

Voracious kūmara moth caterpillars were a dreaded menace. When Rongonui stole the kūmara seeds from his brother Whānui, to impregnate his wife, Whānui was so angry with Rongonui for taking the seeds without his permission that he punished him by sending anuhe, torongū and moko (kūmara moth caterpillars) to destroy the plant's leaves. The pests could appear so suddenly and in such prolific numbers that they were thought to have dropped from the sky.

The most common mode of control was picking the caterpillars off by hand, a task nobody enjoyed. Less hands-on methods included using acrid smoke from smouldering kauri gum or wet kawakawa twigs to destroy the invaders, or encouraging tame karoro or black-backed gulls to feed on the insects.

Young kūmara plants were an attractive snack for hungry kiore (rats) in some areas. Older men would guard the plantations at night, scaring off the rats by shaking rattles made from bunches of mussel shells strung on cords.

The best immature kūmara were harvested when they were three-quarters ripe, before hauhakenga (the main harvest) took place. Their skins were scraped off and the kūmara left to dry in the sun on a paparahi (platform). They were turned each day and put under cover at night. Once dry enough, they were steamed in a hāngi for 12–24 hours. If still not sufficiently dry, they were placed back on the paparahi in the sun, or dried on a rack made from green wooden rods set over live embers. The thoroughly dried result, kao, were stored in kete with mokimoki fern, which imparted a special flavour. The kete would be hung in pātaka (elevated storehouses) for up to two years. If the kao became mouldy before the coming spring, the women who prepared it would be very ashamed.

The main harvest took place in late autumn, before the first frost, during the maramataka of Whānui (Vega or North Star). During the tapu-lifting ceremony, the tohunga would pull up a kūmara plant with leaves and tubers still attached. These would be taken to the sacred place and suspended on a pole or stake as an offering for the atua. Next, a few tubers were dug and cooked – the tohunga would first offer one of the cooked kūmara to the atua, then consume the rest. More kūmara were cooked in a separate oven for the tohunga's assistants, with a larger quantity cooked in a third oven for the rest of the people at the harvest.

After this ceremony, harvesting the crop commenced. Kūmara were carefully dug using kō, wauwau (a pointed digging instrument fashioned from māpara or heartwood) and kāheru (spades). The mature main crop was unearthed carefully so as not to bruise the roots or break their skins. They were then sorted by size and variety; damaged tubers were removed and eaten as soon as possible. The rest were packed into newly made tīraha (flax baskets) and stored in special rua kūmara (underground storage pits) or sometimes in above-ground structures, such as pātaka or whata. Posts supporting the pātaka or whata were often unadorned – any form of carving provided a toehold for hungry kiore intent on reaching the food store.

Rua could store up to 100 tīraha and were meticulously designed to keep kūmara safe and dry. They were generally 1.2 metres deep, with a slanted roof, and looked a bit like small houses buried to the eaves. Drainage was crucial – dampness or water signalled disaster for the crop – so rua were always built on sloping ground, or in a free-draining location, with external and internal drains dug into them. Any shelves cut into the sides and the bottom of the rua were lined with fern

leaf (whekī ponga leaves were particularly well suited). Kūmara were packed in the rua only on sunny, dry days, with each tuber carefully placed in the store to avoid bruising or exposure to dampness. They were checked regularly for rot and turned to ensure they stayed dry. Once filled, the rua was tapu until an important visitor arrived. Only then could the contents be feasted on.

Kūmara were always stored separately from other crops, particularly fern root. As a descendant of Rongo-mā-Tāne, the atua of cultivation and peace, kūmara is associated with peace. Fern root, on the other hand, is a descendant of Haumia-tiketike. It was considered to be a strong, sustaining food suitable for warriors and, as such, linked with warfare. The two foods could not be carried nor stored together.

Yams and taro both coped with being transplanted in the new land, but they were hard to grow and nowhere near as productive as they were back across the Pacific. Uwhi (yams) grew very slowly, taking eight months to mature. Eventually they were replaced when other vegetables, like potatoes, became available. Even though growing uwhi gradually disappeared, its legacy remains in memory through language. Some root crops, such as a red/pink variety of taewa (Māori potato), are referred to by elders as uwhi whero (red yam).

Taro, another staple root crop of the

Pacific Islands, was considered a kai rangatira (food for important people) and thought to be second only to the mighty kūmara. Taro, grown for its stems, leaves and large starchy tubers, was one of early Māori's main crops, even though it took time and effort to grow. Taro need warmth and moisture, so it was planted in rich, damp ground and a layer of sand or gravel was spread on top to retain warmth. Growing taro was easier in Aotearoa's subtropical far north, where up to 10 different varieties were cultivated year round. They were planted in swamps and elaborate drainage systems were built to maintain optimal growing conditions. While most root crops were stored in rua, harvested taro was stored above ground, covered in bracken.

Hue, or bottle gourd, was also widely grown. Hue is believed to have come from Pūtehue, a child of Tāne-mahuta. It was grown mainly for food and for use as water containers, as Māori did not traditionally make or use pottery vessels. A large hue could hold up to 11 litres of water.

Hue were put to a multitude of other uses – as trumpets or flutes, lamps, vessels for shark oil and even as buoys for fishing nets. Pre-planting rituals were performed to ensure this versatile plant would grow well. Hue seeds went through a process called whakarau, in which they were soaked in water and placed in a small basket (kono) containing a mixture of

earth and decayed wood (pōpopo rākau). The soil mixture was covered with leaves or grass and the basket buried in the warm earth near a fire until the seeds sprouted. The seedlings were then ready for planting, but only at the full moon, after another ritual was performed. The person planting them would place a seed in each hand between the thumb and a finger and then face east. He would raise his arms in a big circle in the air, moving them in the shape he wished the gourds to grow. Following this, the two seedlings were planted in the soil. It was only after this that the rest could be planted.

A single hue plant could produce up to 50 fruit. While most of the gourds would eventually become vessels, some were eaten at the kotawa (young) stage of growth, primarily in early summer when other vegetables were in short supply. The first hue of the summer season were put in a hāngi and a karakia recited over the oven, so there would be a good crop later in the season. A branch of karamū was put in the hāngi; the cook would gesture over it as though it was being dug up with a kō. This was done to ensure the hue vines would continue to bear many fruit.

Hue were picked and left to dry when mature, after the rind had hardened and the flesh had dried away. They were usually dried in the sun but other drying methods included baking them by a fire, burying them in warm sand for several months, or shaking pebbles and sand

inside them. Once they were sufficiently dried, women wove flax webbing for carrying and transporting them. Larger hue, which were used to store birds preserved in fat, sometimes had three or four short legs attached at the base. Great care was taken of them – some were even named – and they could be handed down as heirlooms that would last for generations. Some hue were covered with elaborate carvings and decorated with feathers from the birds they contained. These were presented to dignitaries and important guests at feasts.

An old recipe illustrates the hue's usefulness:

Have ready a large calabash decorated with a carved wooden mouth-piece and feathers. Snare your pigeons when the kahikatea berry is ripe, and the birds therefore fat. Remove heads and bones. Roast on wooden spits before a clear fire, arrange flax leaves carefully to convey the fat as it drips from the birds into the calabash. The fat may be kept liquid by means of hot stones. When the birds are roasted, remove the stones from the fat, and place the birds in it, taking care that the fat completely covers them. Close up the mouth of the calabash with a wooden plug, and put by for a rainy day, or a great occasion.

Food of the sea, lakes and rivers

Aotearoa's seemingly endless coastline and countless waterways were an essential source of kai for Māori. Fishing skills were crucial for survival, particularly during winter when other food was difficult to find. Kaimoana – fish, eels, shellfish, crustaceans and sea vegetables – was collected from beaches, waterways and the vast ocean home of Tangaroa.

Men were mostly responsible for fishing out at sea, eeling and diving in deep water for pāua. Women concentrated on gathering shellfish, though they also contributed to the catch by fishing in more sheltered and accessible streams and inlets.

Māori employed sophisticated techniques, involving nets, lines and traps. Each style of fishing had an accompanying body of knowledge about the fishes' habits, the best times and places to fish and the correct ways to catch them. Great respect was accorded to Tangaroa and waterways in general. Before men went onto the sea to fish, karakia would be recited and fishermen would urinate on the net or trap, then sprinkle some on themselves before entering the water. Strict rules were observed on the water; activities such as eating or cutting up freshly caught fish for bait were tapu. Women also observed certain protocols for gathering kaimoana. Trips were made for a specific purpose and only at the appropriate time for harvesting a particular species. Each family and hapū had defined areas within

which they gathered their kaimoana, so they were familiar with where kai could be found. Permission had to be sought from the kaitiaki (guardian) if they wished to gather outside their identified area. Menstruating women were considered tapu, so they couldn't go into the water or gather food. No shellfish could be opened on the reef or over the shellfish beds, or while anyone from a gathering party was in the water. As with agriculture, the maramataka identified the best days and nights for various activities. Experts who knew the movements of various species were consulted and customary law and practices (such as rāhui) honoured.

Māori adapted their traditional fishing equipment to the new conditions: kupenga (net), aho (line), matau (hook), matira (fishing rod), pātia (spear), tāruke (pot), hīnaki (trap) and pā (weir) were all used.

Kupenga were very valuable. Their construction and the area in which they were made was tapu; anyone who breached it risked being slain. Nets were made from harakeke (green flax) and occasionally tī or kiekie (vine). They were made collectively, with each family weaving a part before the pieces were joined together. The mesh (tākekenga), which was formed over bunched fingers, was made tighter and thicker at its centre (called the kōnae), where the strain was the greatest. The upper (kaharunga) and lower (kahararo) ropes of the net were made from undressed flax or tī, which was

more durable than flax. Floats (pōito) of buoyant wood, pumice or gourds were positioned along the top of the net at regular intervals. Using a special netting knot, small mesh bags containing smooth stones (karihi) were attached to the bottom as weights.

Nets were tapu until their first use. The first fish caught in one was often thrown back into the water, or taken to a sacred site while the tohunga recited karakia and offered the fish to Tangaroa.

Nets ranged in size from individual tītoko ika (hand nets) to very large kaharoa (seine nets). Some were 1.6 kilometres long and required up to 500 handlers. After each use, nets were dried, folded and stored away on a platform or in a regular storehouse (whata) raised on piles. Large, funnel-shaped nets (ahuriri or riritai), up to 25 metres long and 7.5 metres in diameter, were designed for tidal rivers and could catch up to 450 kilograms of fish at a time. In rocky areas, where kaharoa or ahuriri could not be used, fishermen with wooden poles would direct fish into matarau (circular hoop nets) or kōrapa (long-handled scoop nets) in a method known as kōkō (prodding the fish with a pole).

Not all nets were large – small hand-held nets, some of which were fastened to poles, were also used. Kupenga (a very fine-meshed, long, conical net fastened to a frame) was used for catching īnanga (whitebait). Other small nets (toemi) had openings that drew together like a bag, trapping the fish inside.

Line fishing – using extremely strong, dressed flax fibre twisted into a cord – was widely practised. Fish hooks were made from a variety of materials, including wood, bone, stone or shell. There were two principal types: a traditional matau (suspended hook) for catching bottom-dwelling fish; and trolling lures for catching kahawai and mangā (barracuda). Matau were large and distinctively shaped, with the point very close to the hook shank. These were typically carved from bone, but wooden hooks were also used to catch parrotfish, cod, tarakihi, moki and snapper. Wooden hooks were made by training growing plants and young trees, such as tauhinu (cottonwood shrub) or mangemange (climbing fern), into the desired shape. The hooks were harvested after they had matured and become rigid, then heat-treated in hot earth, beneath a fire. Trolling lures were made of composite materials and often included wood, bone, shell or stone shanks, with a short, pointed, bone barb lashed to the end. Kahawai lures were decorated with tufts of kiwi, kōtare (kingfisher) or kororā (little blue penguin) feathers instead of being baited. Others were slightly curved and inlaid with pāua, so they would spin and reflect light from the iridescent shell when they were trolled through the water behind a canoe.

Tuna (freshwater eels) were another key food source – Māori had more than 100 names to describe their different colours and sizes. Te hopu tuna (eeling) could be done by hand or by using weirs, pots and spears. The pā tuna (eel weir) was commonly used in rivers, streams and the outlets of lagoons and lakes. Most pā tuna were pā tauremu: two hardwood (usually mānuka) fences that progressively channelled the eels into a hīnaki tuna (basket trap). Some weirs were up to 370 metres long. Women wove hīnaki tuna from flax and vines, creating an ingenious design with a funnel neck at the mouth of a large elliptical basket. There was no way out for tuna once they'd passed in through the funnel.

Tuna were also caught in hīnaki without using a weir. Bait (often worms) would be placed in the bottom of the basket in a small vessel called a pū toke, which looked like a miniature hīnaki, or in a flax bag called a tōrehe, thus luring the eels to swim into the trap. Eels were also hunted in the dark using a rama (torch flare) and a matarau (spear) or hand net. Toi, or bobbing, was another means of nocturnal eeling. Worms or grubs were threaded onto a string made of flax or tī leaves, which was then attached to the end of a stick. When the tuna's teeth caught on the fibres, it was either swung ashore or caught using a spear. Eels could even be caught by hand. Once caught, tuna were gutted, cleaned and dried, then hung in a storehouse or packed into baskets to be stored. Live tuna – up to 300 at a time – could be kept and fed in korotete (eel cages) or in ponds or lagoons with no outlets until they were needed.

Skilled fishermen used barbed spears to catch flounder, stingrays and sunfish. Spears were used to hunt porpoises, while larger harpoons were used on dolphins and sharks.

Other kaimoana, such as kōura (crayfish), were caught using tāruke – round baskets woven from thin branches of mānuka and kareao (supplejack) that were similar in design to hīnaki tuna. Although tāruke had a funnel entrance like hīnaki tuna, the opening was much larger and set at the top of the pot. A small piece of netted fabric called a kōrohe or puhatero was attached at the funnel neck to prevent the crayfish escaping. Pāua or pātangaroa (starfish) were used as crayfish bait, or kāweru. This was placed in the pot with a few stone sinkers, then lowered by rope to the seafloor and a float attached to mark its whereabouts. Fishermen often located kōura in shallow depths by feeling around with their feet, then plucking them from the water by hand. Freshwater crayfish, which are much smaller than their oceanic counterparts, were caught by lowering bundles of bracken onto the river or lake floor. After a few hours, the branches would be pulled up with crayfish clinging to the branches. Māori took advantage of kanae (grey mullet) entering tidal rivers in large numbers, startling them so they leapt into nearby canoes. As

a result, the fish are known as 'the leaping sons of Tangaroa'.

Shellfish were another important food source. Māori harvested and ate more than 27 types, most of which were collected by hand. Sometimes a ripi (knife) was used to detach them from the rocks; other times the rake-like rou kākahi. This tool had a rōrī (net) attached to catch molluscs as they were raked up. Freshwater mussels were also gathered in this way. Various types of rimu or rimurimu (red and green seaweed) were picked to eat. Karengo was harvested from tidal rocks in winter and spring, then dried immediately to stop it from going mouldy. Dried karengo was a crucial protein source in winter.

In the South Island, rimurapa (bull kelp) was also harvested. Rimurapa was used primarily to form pōhā (vessels) for preserving food in rendered fat (especially tītī or muttonbird). To make pōhā, the harvested rimurapa was first opened by thrusting a hand down the middle of the kelp, then it was blown up into a bag. A piece of flax was used to tie the end and the kelp was hung in the sun to dry. Pōhā were also used for whakawhiti kaimoana – a means of propagating seafood in which kaimoana such as live shellfish, starfish or pāua would be put in pōhā and transported to a new area. After arriving at the new location, the pōhā would be lowered into the sea. Slits made in the bags would open up, allowing the sea creatures to escape into the new waters to breed and

Man splitting rods of vine. McDonald, James Ingram, 1865-1935. Photographs. Ref: PA1-q-257-07-3. Alexander Turnbull Library, Wellington, New Zealand.

attract more of their species.

Although used primarily for pōhā, rimurapa could also be eaten – the blade of the plant was roasted and chewed.

Food of the sky

Much of what Māori ate came from the plants of the forest, their cultivated lands and the sea. Animals as a food source were limited in variety, by comparison, but they were plentiful. Māori developed inspired ways to capture the proteins of the land and skies.

There were no terrestrial mammals in Aotearoa before the first waka arrived carrying the kiore (Polynesian rat) and kurī (Polynesian dog). In the absence of predators, birds had taken over. Some, like the flightless moa, grew unusually large. Māori found more than nine different moa species roaming the land. The giant birds had many uses besides being a bountiful source of meat and eggs: their eggshells were used to carry water; and their bones were carved into fish hooks, harpoon heads, spears and pendants. Moa feathers and skins were used for ornamental purposes and clothing. The enormous creatures were an easy target for hunters' spears and traps, and they are believed to have been hunted to extinction many hundreds of years ago. Their demise meant that other indigenous birds, as well as the kiore and kurī, became crucial sources of protein.

Kiore were considered a gourmet treat, despite their small size. The rats were hunted from late autumn into winter, when they were fat from a summer of gorging themselves on forest fruit. Kiore were nocturnal, hiding in ground holes or tree trunks during the day. When they moved between feeding grounds, kiore travelled single file along tops of ridges on paths that became worn smooth by their feet. Māori exploited this evidence of their movements to track and capture them. Kiore hunting was well organised, with ara kiore (rat tracks) lined with tāwhiti kiore (rat traps) to catch them as they foraged. Māori used two categories of kiore traps: spring traps containing various forms of sprung snares, and pit traps. Spring traps were made from mānuka bark, aka kareao (supplejack vine) and muka (a type of flax fibre), with various mechanisms that were activated when the kiore took the bait (usually kūmara or berries).

When the rat entered the tāwhiti, it triggered a spring which caught it in a snare and trapped or strangled it. Alternatively, kiore hunters would dig a pit trap and suspend berries from sticks laid over the opening. When the kiore walked across the stick to get the bait, it fell into the trap. Kiore were either skinned and eaten right away (fire-roasted or cooked in the hāngi) or preserved in gourds or pōhā in their own fat. Kiore huahua (preserved rat) was a delicacy that was saved for visitors, often forming

a kind of currency at special occasions. Other species of rats introduced with the arrival of Pākehā created competition for resources and the kiore eventually declined.

Kurī thrived in Aotearoa and could weigh up to 15 kilograms. They were considered both valuable hunting companions and a culinary luxury imbued with tapu and ritual. Several places – including the Tūtaekurī River in Hawke's Bay – were named after events where kurī was feasted on. Tūtaekurī means dog offal: the scraps from a feast that was ordered by chief Hikawera were thrown into the river afterwards. Kurī were used to hunt kiwi, kākāpō, weka, pūkeko and māunu (moulting grey ducks). To catch kiwi, a hunter would attract the birds by imitating their cry. When the kiwi was close enough, the kurī would be let loose to catch it. Others used kurī to catch pūkeko, which were not strong fliers. Beaters would flush the birds out of the swamp into strong northwest winds. Pūkeko would quickly tire, making it easy for the kurī to catch them.

Birds were caught using specially designed snares, decoys and lures. Most birds were taken between May and July, though weka could be caught as early as April in the South Island.

Plump kererū, kākā and tūī were caught in the summer, after they had feasted on tawa berries and rātā nectar. Scouts kept careful watch on birds' food supplies months before the main season, so that hunters could be advised when the time was right. The first bird killed by each hunter was always offered back to Tāne. Hunters were careful not to leave loose feathers behind, believing it would frighten the birds away. The only bird Māori did not take for food was the huia – it was tapu as its distinctive feathers were associated with the heads of chiefs.

Hunters often attracted birds by using pepe (leaves) to imitate their cries. Different leaves were used depending on the species – harakeke for weka, and manono or patatē for tūī. Trained decoys enticed gregarious kākā to their deaths. A pet kākā would be tethered to the base of a pole with a pōria (a leg ring carved from human bone, whalebone, bird bones or pounamu) and trained to screech to attract fellow birds while the hunter hid behind a fern screen. When a wild kākā approached, the hunter would hit it with a stick, catch it with a noose or grab it by hand. This method was also used to catch tūī, hihi, korimako, tīeke, kōkako and tātaihore, with the perch often set up by water to lure thirsty birds.

Observing birds' habits was key to catching them. Kererū loved to eat miro berries, which made them thirsty. Hunters capitalised on this by placing waka manu or waka kererū (water-filled wooden troughs) in or on miro tree trunks. Snares were set once the birds were used to drinking from the waka manu. Up to 200 kererū a day could be caught by the tutu method, where a hunter would sit on a platform set in the branches of a fruit or berry tree. Artificial tumu (perches) were placed on the ends of short poles lashed into position. Noose snares were spread on the perches and the hunter held the ends. When a bird landed on the perch, the snares were pulled.

Māori also caught kererū and other birds by hand, by spear and with traps. Spears were made from tawa, kāpara or aka (stems of climbing plants) and were fashioned with a tara (barbed point) made of bone (often human), hardwood, stingray spine or pounamu. These spears were so long and cumbersome that they had to be dragged on the ground. Barbed spears were carved to hunt perching birds like tūī and kākā, while maiere (short spears) were about 3–4 metres long and made to take birds from small trees or shrubs. Long spears (tao kaihua or taoroa) were used to hunt birds perched in tall trees. The hunter would rest the 6–11-metre-long spear on a branch and wait until the bird was close enough.

No tools were needed to catch tūī in the colder months. The birds would often stay in poroporo shrubs overnight, feeding on winter-ripe fruit. Just before dawn, with the light of burning torches, men would climb the trees to the tūī's perches. The birds' claws would be so contracted with cold that they couldn't let go and fly away. Hunters could pluck them from the perch by hand or shake the tree until the tūī fell out.

Many species fell prey to snares and two main methods were used: tākiri and tāhei. Tākiri employed a single snare in a perch – a quick tug by the hunter would trap the bird by the feet. Three different snares – mutu, tumu and pewa – worked this way. The mutu snare was used both on the ground and in trees. The mutu was made from a single piece of carved wood in an L- or T-shape, with a horizontal perch and a vertical jamb. A looped snare was draped over the mutu before the trap was placed in the tree. When a bird landed on the horizontal perch, the noose-like snare was tugged and the bird was trapped against the upright jamb. This allowed the hunter to lower the bird before killing it and resetting the trap. Mutu were used in miro, hīnau, maire, kahikatea, tawai, rātā and rimu trees.

Tumu snares were used in small trees or shrubs. Unlike the man-made mutu, a tumu comprised a small branch divided into two and tied together at the end, which was left growing in the tree or shrub. A snare loop with a cord was laid on top. When a bird landed on it, the waiting hunter tugged on the cord and trapped his prey. The snared bird would be removed from the tumu and tethered to a peg stuck in the ground so the hunter could continue trapping.

The pewa was used in a similar fashion, but a lure of ripe berries or nectar-bearing flowers would be tied to the perch. Tūī, for example, were taken in snares baited with rātā flowers.

While mutu, tumu and pewa snares required the hunter to be present, the tāhei method was hands-free. Under this system, a series of slip-knotted snares were attached to a cord or rod suspended between two branches, and birds were caught by their necks. The nooses tightened as they struggled to get free. These snares were generally cleared and reset twice daily. They were effective on many types of birds but would be ripped apart by the kākā's sharp beaks.

Seabirds were taken along the coastlines, most famously the tītī (muttonbird, or sooty shearwater petrel). In times past, tītī breeding grounds extended from offshore islands to high hills far inland. As the sun set, nesting tītī would return to their burrows and breeding grounds. Returning tītī would swoop low over the cliffs, where hunters lay waiting for them with a large net strung between two poles and a fire burning behind it to attract the birds. When the birds flew towards the fire, they were caught in the net. It was a bad omen if the first bird struck one of the supporting poles, and no further birds would be taken. If the first bird struck the net, the hunt would be successful.

Other seabirds, such as albatrosses, seagulls and mollymawks, were caught with wooden hooks with bone barbs. The hook was baited and the birds were trolled for, similar to fishing.

KAI MĀORI COOKING METHODS

Hāngi

Putting down a hāngi is a serious business, requiring a high degree of organisation, preparation, fortitude and patience. In the 21st century, a hāngi is a major event – a style of cooking used for celebrations, family gatherings or other important occasions. For early Māori, cooking in an underground earth oven was a way of life they'd always practised. Hāngi were prepared largely by women while the men were hunting, with the food ready for the evening meal. Any leftovers, particularly vegetables, were eaten the next morning.

At its most basic, a hāngi is an underground steam oven. The food – wrapped in leaves or in woven baskets – is flavoured by smoke from the initial fire, the surrounding earth and the native plants used. Then, as now, the size of the hāngi pit (umu) varied depending on the number of people being cooked for and what was being cooked in it. Archaeologists have discovered huge umu in the South Island that may have been used to cook seals or moa. Usually, pits were much smaller – around a metre in

diameter and up to half a metre deep. Each family had their own pit and would reuse it.

To begin, a fire was carefully laid in the pit, with wood layered on until level with the opening. Special stones – ideally volcanic rocks, which withstand high temperatures, rather than sedimentary river stones that can shatter – were set on top. A hāngi fire needed to burn for at least an hour or two (depending on the size of the pit) to sufficiently heat the stones through so they held enough heat to cook the food when the hāngi was sealed. This part of the process cannot be rushed. Sometimes stones were heated in the ordinary cooking fire (adjacent to the pit) rather than in a separate fire laid in the pit.

After the fire had been burning solidly for an hour or two, the bottom of the pit would be a sea of wood ash and white-hot stones. At this point, any unburnt wood would be removed and water sprinkled over the stones to wash away leftover ashes (ashes left in a hāngi taint the taste of the food). The stones were levelled out and a woven band of harakeke, called a pae umu, was inserted into the pit to

keep the food together and away from the earthen walls. Vegetation such as fern fronds was placed on top.

Any food to be cooked was wrapped in leaves and placed within the pae umu. Hard, dense or tough foods, like taro, for example, would take longer to steam than fish, so they would be placed closer to the hot stones. Aromatic greens would be used to flavour the vegetables or meat. Once the food was in, the hāngi was covered with more vegetation and woven matting. Finally, earth was piled on top to seal in the steam. A small hāngi might steam for two or three hours; a larger one might take twice as long. Constant vigilance was needed to ensure no steam escaped from the pit. A hāngi that was lifted too soon was a huge waste of resources, both in terms of food and people power.

In geothermal areas of New Zealand, particularly around Rotorua and Taupō, Māori could harness the natural steam vents to prepare hāngi without the need for fire. Instead, they would dig holes in the ground and use the natural steam to cook their food. This method is still used in the area today.

Hāngi methods were also used for long-term cooking as well as preparing the next meal. Hard, fibrous vegetables, such as the turnip-like rearea, were dried and then cooked in a hāngi for 24 hours, wrapped in various leaves and ferns for flavour. When they were removed from the pit, the rearea were dried again before being stored. Freshly dug kūmara were wrapped in kūmara vine or pūriri leaves and baked in an earth oven for 24 hours, then sun-dried for a fortnight before eating.

Hāngi preparation evolved with the advent of more sophisticated tools and a greater variety of ingredients. A contemporary hāngi, for example, will be dug with shovels. The rocks might be collected from a garden centre, rather than painstakingly gathered. The food will be packed in wire baskets, and wet sacking or newspaper laid on top in place of woven mats. But the core principles remain. Indigenous plants are still used – puka leaves will be used to line wire baskets, while kawakawa and horopito continue to be key flavour-givers. Food cooked in a hāngi, whether in woven harakeke kono or repurposed wire baskets, is smoky and earthy, with a freshness from the powerful aromatics and vegetation.

Open-fire cooking

Compared to the laborious and time-consuming work involved in preparing a hāngi, cooking over an open fire was easy and efficient. Fires could be laid anywhere, as long as there was a steady supply of fuel nearby.

While the tools required for making fire were portable and usually easy to find, successful fire-lighting took skills that people today would find hard to master.

To start a fire, the fire-lighter would need to create enough friction between the kauahi (a flat, grooved piece of wood) and the hika (a pointed stick) to ignite a spark that would set alight a pile of dried leaves or twigs.

When it came to cooking, fires were used mostly for grilling. Fish or birds would be speared on sticks and set over hot stones or embers, or set above them on a rack made from mānuka.

As well as cooking over flames, open fires were used for other methods. A range of ingredients – including tuna (eels), vegetables and 'cakes' of pounded fern root – could be wrapped in harakeke or other leaves and left to bake in the hot ashes. Small birds could be coated in a paste of clay and baked in the same way. If boiling was required, stones would be heated in the fire, then dropped into a calabash or gourd containing water or fat and the food to be cooked or reheated.

Preserving, smoking and dehydrating

Preserving food, whether by covering it in fat, smoking or dehydrating, was an essential skill in Aotearoa. Since the seasons dictated that there were fewer harvests than in the tropical Pacific Islands, Māori developed various ways to ensure they had enough supplies stored away for the winter.

Open fires, or their carefully tended embers, were useful when it came to preserving fish or eels. An ahi rara tuna (eel-drying fire) allowed Māori to preserve a large number of eels at once. After being cleaned and boned, the eels would be skewered on stripped sticks or fern stalks, then propped up to grill over a long bed of embers. When they were cooked through, they were cooled and hung up or packed in pātaka set above the ground. Fish were dried in a similar way, over an ahi rara ika (fish-drying fire).

Smouldering embers were used to smoke fish and birds, both to impart flavour and finish the dehydrating process. Mānuka, a long-burning hardwood with a distinctive aroma, was the wood of choice. While open-fire smoking was the best way to smoke large quantities, small catches could be smoked by placing embers in a small hole, hanging the fish or birds over them, then covering the hole with a damp mat. In this method, the smoke stays inside the hole even when the embers die out.

Māori who lived in places with a reliably dry climate could skip the fire and hang gutted and boned fish or eels to dry in the sun and wind. Tiny īnanga (whitebait) could also be sun-dried, along with berries, seaweed, shark and some vegetables. For larger fish or eels, often a combination of methods would be used – an initial part-cook over embers, then the fish or eels would be finished by hanging in the sun or over a smouldering, smoky fire for several days. The dried results were

hung in pātaka, where a constant airflow prevented them from getting damp and going off.

Preserving birds was a major task. Methods varied between regions. While smaller birds were usually eaten fresh, larger ones were plucked, cleaned and boned before being chilled in cold water. They were then dried and cooked over flames on a spit, with the fat collected in wooden troughs. When the birds were cooked, they were transferred to gourds or containers made of bark or wood. The rendered fat was heated until boiling (using hot stones) then poured over the cooked birds until they were covered. When the fat had set, the preserved birds would be stored away for future eating. Alternatively, birds could be cooked in

boiling water then packed into gourds and covered in fat.

Preserving tītī came with its own process. The birds were cooked in their own fat, then stored in inflated bags made from bull kelp, which were in turn stored in specially made flax kete as a final protective layer. The kelp bags were carefully sun-dried to preserve them first, before they were put into service. Tītī preserved in this way could be stored for up to three years. Some pōhā were large enough that they could hold up to 300 tītī. Pōhā were also used to preserve seals. The seals were prepared in a similar way to tītī and buried in the sand at the seashore, where they would keep almost indefinitely.

Precious kūmara could be preserved, too. The young tubers were scraped and

Mrs S Burke placing bark around kelp/flax bags of salted mutton birds, at Solomon Island. Ref: PAColl-6001-58. Alexander Turnbull Library, Wellington, New Zealand.

sun-dried, making them instantly portable and handy for travelling. When it came to longer-term storage, kūmara were kept in a rua pit – a kind of covered underground cave – to keep them in good condition through winter or times of scarcity.

Fermentation

Fermentation was as popular with early Māori as it is with modern food-lovers, both for reasons of prolonged storage and for the intense, funky flavours. In the right conditions, fermentation encourages the growth of beneficial bacteria and prevents 'bad' bacteria from spoiling the food. Fermenting changes the texture and flavour of foods, often in delicious (if strong-smelling) ways.

To make kōura mara (fermented crayfish), Māori placed crayfish in woven flax kete and left them submerged in streams or slow-running rivers until the flesh was soft and coming away from the shell. This method was also used with fish. Later, after Europeans introduced sweetcorn, the same methods were used to make kānga kōpiro. Corn cobs were put into kete or sacks and left to ferment in running water for up to six weeks. The kernels were stripped from the cobs and mashed into a kind of hummus-like porridge (kānga pirau) that could be eaten hot or cold. This fermented product, with its pungent smell (in 1964, writer Riki Erihi described it as 'an unholy

fragrance'), is an acquired taste, but fans love it.

The development of rēwena parāoa (Māori bread) was a much more conventionally palatable form of fermentation. After flour was introduced by European settlers, Māori used cooked potatoes to make a pre-ferment 'starter' to leaven their bread dough. Rēwena bread has a distinctive sweet-sourness, similar to sourdough, and the longer the starter is kept the more the flavour develops.

WHERE THERE IS KAI, THERE IS MANAAKITANGA

Ka mau tonu ngā taonga tapu o ngā
mātua tūpuna
Koinei ngā taonga i tuku iho, nā te atua
Hold fast to the treasures of the ancestors
For they are the treasures handed down to
us by the gods

The kai has been grown and gathered and
the rua are full. We have remembered the
past to look to the future. We have given
thanks to and honoured the atua and
those who have come before us. Now is
the time to share and enjoy our kai in the
enduring spirit of manaakitanga.

As it was with the ancestors, as it is now,
it's with integrity, sincerity and respect
that we welcome our guests to share our
kai. We extend our welcoming spirit and
aroha to those who join us at the table.
Through this, we build our unity through
the act of giving and sharing.

Kia tāku whānau, me ngā hoa, mō te kai
Kia ora
For our family, friends and food
We say thank you

2—

THE INGREDIENTS

He whā tāwhara ki uta,
he kiko tāmure ki tai

The flowers of the kiekie
on the land, the flesh of the
snapper in the sea

NGĀ TIPU:
INDIGENOUS PLANTS

ARUHE
Bracken root
Pteridium esculentum
LOCATED: ACROSS AOTEAROA

Traditionally known by Māori as aruhe or rārahu, bracken is a tenacious fern that loves warmer climates. Given the chance, it will take over deforested areas, abandoned farmlands and bare hillsides. Today the fern has spread to most parts of New Zealand, and is also present in Australia, but some argue that it wasn't always so common. Māori might have aided its vigorous proliferation when they started clearing lowland forests.

Māori have used the fern for centuries. Aruhe is considered a sign of perseverance and has earned quite a reputation in tradition and mythology. In Ngāti Porou legend, the early ancestor Toi lived by eating the fern and other wild foods like tī kōuka and mamaku. Ngāti Pāoa tell a story about how their ancestor Pāoa didn't like offering the fern to guests or visitors; he believed it should instead be kept as a last resort for times of scarcity.

The starchy bracken root was harvested in late winter and early spring. These rhizomes were roasted and ground for flour to make a kind of bread. Young, unfurled shoots were eaten, too.

Aruhe also had medicinal and practical uses. In small doses, it was used to cure diarrhoea, or as an antidote for seasickness. Wearing a small piece around the neck was thought to protect you from headaches and colds. Aruhe compresses or bandages were sometimes used to ease aches and pains, and the ashes of burnt fronds were applied to severe burns. In villages, fronds were used to line rua and the stalks were used to line large whare.

Te Arawa and the Ngāti Tūwharetoa iwi used to carpet lake beds with aruhe to attract and catch colonies of kōura – an ancient method that's still incredibly efficient.

HAKEKE
Wood-ear mushroom
Auricularia polytricha
LOCATED: LOWLAND FORESTS ACROSS
AOTEAROA

For the most part, Māori weren't big mushroom eaters. While several varieties of mushrooms thrive in Aotearoa, only hakeke was used as a food source, during times of scarcity. Hakeke (see page 70, top right) can be found growing on deadwood in lowland forest during early spring and late autumn. It has a subtle, woody flavour that is quickly lost during the cooking process, but it absorbs flavours very well and is excellent for broths and stocks. Hakeke can be eaten raw but their tough texture makes them better suited to sautéing or slow-cooking methods.

HARAKEKE (flowers, seeds)
New Zealand flax
Phormium tenax
LOCATED: ACROSS AOTEAROA

It's hard to imagine how Māori might've survived without the strength and versatility of harakeke (see page 70, bottom left and right). There was a famous encounter between Māori chiefs and the 19th-century missionary William Colenso, in which he advised them that harakeke didn't grow in England. They replied, 'How is it possible to live without it?' Their concerns were understandable, considering harakeke was used in almost every facet of pre-contact Māori life.

Harakeke was the fibre of Aotearoa, used for clothing, fishing nets, medicine, ropes and food, among many other purposes. Medicinally, harakeke was used to treat everything from toothaches to menstrual cramps. The gum was used as an aid for chafed skin and for healing wounds. It could also be rolled up and placed into a tooth cavity, working as a filling of sorts. The root was chewed, or boiled and turned into an elixir to remedy dysentery, lacerations and bleeding bowels.

Harakeke was also used as a means for communicating the past. It's an ancient Polynesian belief that the weaver is a channel through whom the gods communicate. Intricate patterns in woven articles told stories of our ancestors – their whakapapa, their beliefs, their journeys. These would be passed on from one generation to the next, keeping alive the spiritual values of those who came before us.

I have taken the time over the past few years to learn how to make rourou, a small basket in which food is cooked and served. Rourou is also a symbol of manaakitanga; it's something you fill with kai and share with whānau and manuhiri (visitors) to the marae.

Harakeke produces three food sources: seeds, flowers and nectar. The red bloom

of harakeke bursts into life between October and February. Wai kōrari (flax honey) is found at the base of the flowers. To extract it, the flowers are harvested then tapped upside down over a small calabash to capture the liquid contents. The petals themselves are sweet and can be eaten.

As summer goes by and the flowers disappear, the rich brown pods clustering at the end of the harakeke branches start producing seeds that are ready to harvest by April. A single pod contains dozens of small black seeds that can be used in a variety of ways, such as sprinkling them onto salads or bread, or eating straight from the pod. At Hiakai, we toast the seeds and use them in our smoked chocolate truffles.

HĪNAU (berries)
Elaeocarpus dentatus
LOCATED: LOWLAND FORESTS ACROSS AOTEAROA

Hīnau berries (above left) were one of the very few berries that Māori consumed. They grow on towering trees, which can grow 20 metres high and are covered in distinctive dark green, almost waxy-looking leaves.

Every spring, the trees grow clusters of goblet-shaped white flowers, streaked with pink and yellow. By the time summer rolls in, the hīnau's branches are laden with berries that resemble olives.

Māori used hīnau berries to prepare a laborious delicacy. They were pounded, then sifted through special baskets called hītari to make a mealy pulp. A paste from that pulp was used to bake large cakes in hāngi. The finished cakes, dark in colour, were then stored and cured in pools of water for months. Modern research shows that the berries' seeds are a good source of fatty acids.

Māori used a concoction of hīnau bark to treat skin ailments. There are also reports that Māori created and applied a dark brown 'lacquer' made from the bark to reinforce boats and canoes. Today, fire-retardant hīnau timber is used in the furniture-making industry.

HOROPITO
Pepper tree
Pseudowintera colorata
LOCATED: LOWLAND FORESTS IN THE NORTH ISLAND AND UPPER SOUTH ISLAND

Horopito's crimson-speckled leaves (see page 72, right) pack a peppery punch. The tree, which is closely related to kawakawa, was traditionally used for medicinal purposes. Its healing properties were so reliable that it was nicknamed 'bushman's painkiller'. Horopito's antifungal properties make it a perfect natural remedy for ringworm and other skin complaints. Māori would bruise the leaves and branches then soak them in water to create a lotion that would be applied to the affected area.

A simple tea brewed from horopito and water was drunk to treat a stomachache and oral thrush. Chewing on the leaves had a numbing effect, ideal for easing toothache.

Horopito was said to be a useful replacement for quinine: Suzanne Aubert, a French nun who spent the majority of her life in New Zealand, incorporated the ingredient into her patent medicine, Karana, late in the 1800s.

Today, horopito is more commonly used for seasoning. I enjoy its versatility and the way it adds depth to both sweet and savoury dishes; it's a must-have in the Hiakai pantry. The fresh leaves can be used to spice up soups, stocks and sauces. At Hiakai, we often steep the leaves in cream overnight, which is then used to make salted caramel petits fours. The leaves are also dehydrated and ground into flakes to add to spice rubs or to simply season food in place of ground black pepper.

HUE
Gourd
Lagenaria siceraria
LOCATED: UPPER NORTH ISLAND

Hue is a gourd plant that used to have multiple uses in everyday Māori life. In Māori mythology, hue takes the personified form of the goddess Hinepūtēhue, the youngest daughter of

Tāne and Hinerauamoa. After Ranginui and Papatūānuku were separated, Hinepūtēhue is said to have captured the fury of the gods in her gourds of love.

The hue was cultivated extensively in Aotearoa's northern regions, where the warmer climate helped them thrive. The ideal time for harvesting hue to eat was in the middle of summer, when the skin and flesh of the young fruit is soft.

Hue were traditionally cooked in a hāngi but the young fruit is also enjoyed raw. It's still edible when mature but the skin will be very thick and the flesh takes on a dry, almost floury texture when overripe.

KAMOKAMO
Heirloom squash
Cucurbita pepo
LOCATED: ACROSS AOTEAROA

Summer brings long-awaited crops of kamokamo (see page 75), which belongs to the same family as pumpkin, marrow, zucchini and squash. Kamokamo is thought to have been introduced to Aotearoa by early European settlers in the 19th century. Māori loved this vegetable so much that it was given status as a taonga crop, meaning that it is highly prized and protected by Rongo-mā-Tāne, the god of cultivated foods.

Kamokamo's outer skin varies in colour, from deep green with pale yellow specks to a burnt orange speckled green. It's usually harvested while very young, when the flesh is at its sweetest.

Young kamokamo suits dry cooking methods that bring out its best flavour. At Hiakai, we slowly cook kamokamo in our woodfire, layering it with a soy mirin glaze as it roasts. We allow the flesh to lightly char, which adds a beautiful smokiness. Each season, I make a couple of jars of kamokamo kimchi to enjoy throughout the year. The flowers are also edible and can be used in the same way as zucchini flowers.

Fully mature kamokamo becomes very similar to its relative, the much larger marrow. The high water content of mature kamokamo makes it best suited for making soups or purées.

KARAKA, KŌPĪ (berries)
Corynocarpus laevigatus
LOCATED: COASTAL FORESTS. HIGHLY ABUNDANT IN TARANAKI

Karaka berries (see page 76, left) are notorious for being lethal in the wrong hands. The bright orange fruit tends to catch the eye of dogs and young children, who can become gravely ill if they eat the inner seed. The fresh seeds of karaka berries contain a poisonous alkaloid called karakin, which must be removed before they're safe to eat.

I insist that anyone wishing to try their

hand at cooking karaka berries do so with the utmost care. Do not leave the berries in an area that is easily accessible to children or pets, as the consequences could be fatal.

The first step is to roast the berries at a high heat for approximately one hour to start breaking down the flesh. Next, cook the berries for a *minimum of 12 hours* in a hāngi pit to further break down the outer flesh and begin destroying the karakin inside the seed. If you don't have access to a hāngi pit, cooking the berries in a pot of simmering water will suffice (you'll have to periodically top up the water as they cook). Once the berries have cooked for 12 hours, transfer them to a container. Cover with water and leave to steep overnight. The next morning, rub the berries together to remove any remaining

flesh (it should easily fall away). I suggest wearing gloves when doing this.

When all the flesh has been removed, place the seeds in a container. Cover with cold water and leave to soak overnight. The next day, drain the seeds, then cover again with cold water and leave to soak overnight again. Repeat this process for seven days. At the end of the seven days, the karaka seeds are ready to eat.

Traditionally, the treated seeds would be dehydrated in the sun and stored away for the months when food was scarce. When the time came, the seeds would be pounded down to make flour, then mixed with water and cooked on coals like flatbread.

KARAMŪ (leaves and berries)
Coprosma robusta
LOCATED: LOWLAND FORESTS ACROSS
AOTEAROA

Karamū (see page 76, right) is one of our
most abundant and under-utilised natural
treasures. Māori used the sacred plant in
a variety of ways; tohunga used it at birth
ceremonies and child naming ceremonies,
and branches would be held over a sick
person while a karakia was performed,
asking the gods to return them to full
health.

Karamū is a member of the coffee
family. Early European settlers roasted the
seeds and mixed them with boiling water
for karamū coffee. The plant's bright
orange berries, which can be eaten straight
off the tree, were a favourite bush snack
for Māori children. The juice of these
berries is richly coloured, and Māori used
it to dye harakeke.

Karamū can ordinarily be found in
areas of native bush near streams, where
it gets plenty of sunlight. Another sign to
look for is orange patches on the forest
floor speckled with small seeds; this is a
result of birds and lizards snacking on the
berries and spitting out the seeds.

Each berry contains two tiny seeds;
removing them can be a laborious process
but the end result is worth it. After
picking berries, the best technique is to
push them through a fine-mesh sieve. The
resulting juice can be used in dressings,
oil and vinegar infusions, or to flavour ice
creams and sorbets.

Māori harvested karamū's thick, glossy
leaves and juvenile shoots to make herbal
tea, which was an effective treatment for
inflammation and bladder problems. At
Hiakai, we make tea from the leaves then
chill it and combine it with our house-
made Karamū Vinegar to make Karamū
Vinaigrette (see pages 152 and 252).

KAREAO
Supplejack, bush asparagus
Ripogonum scandens
LOCATED: LOWLAND FORESTS ACROSS
AOTEAROA

Kareao is a native vine; its name means
'twisted rope'. Anyone who loves to
explore the great New Zealand outdoors
has probably tripped up once or twice on
this coiled wonder. The thick black vine
crawls along the forest floor until it finds a
tree to climb, then wraps itself around the
trunk and branches on a mission to reach
the forest canopy.

According to Māori mythology, Māui
sought revenge on the eel god, Tunaroa,
after the deity knocked over and insulted
Māui's wife as she gathered water from
a stream. Māui ambushed Tunaroa, and
brutally hacked him to death. Tunaroa
was cut into three: the head was tossed
into the sea and became saltwater eels; the
tail was thrown into the river and became

freshwater eels; and the very tip of the tail was thrown into the forest, where it became the kareao vine.

Kareao played an important role in the everyday lives of Māori. The long, dense vines were used in the construction of houses, waka, baskets, fences, eel traps and crayfish nets. For medicine, Māori peeled away the kareao root's outer layer and ground it to a pulp, then left it to steep in water. When it was drunk, this concoction was said to alleviate fevers and treat blood disorders, bowel complaints, scabies and secondary symptoms of syphilis. Pregnant women beware – the same concoction was used to procure abortion.

The young shoots are similar in appearance and taste to asparagus. Thanks to their high water content (and delicious taste when raw), the young shoots are the perfect bush snack. Māori also used to steam them in a hāngi until completely tender.

Foraging for kareao is best done in winter or early summer, when damp soil and tree bark has allowed new shoots to grow. Finding kareao shoots requires a keen eye – they're hard to spot among the tangled skeins of mature vines. I've personally spent an entire day in the forest with the sole purpose of collecting kareao shoots, only to find myself going home empty-handed. When I do strike gold and manage to gather several dozen in one hit, I take them back to the restaurant where we pickle them to prolong their shelf life.

KAWAKAWA (leaves, berries)
Piper excelsum
LOCATED: THROUGHOUT THE NORTH ISLAND, TOP HALF OF THE SOUTH

Kawakawa (see page 78) is probably the most used herb in the Māori pātaka (pantry). The tree is considered sacred and plays an important role in many aspects of Māori life. Kawakawa is a symbol of both birth and death, and is used for sprinkling water in purification rituals. Historically, placing a leaf or sprig of kawakawa beneath a woman or between her breasts prior to intercourse was thought to aid conception. Kawakawa leaves and branches play an important role on marae: branches are waved to welcome visitors and the leaves are woven into a wreath to be worn around the head at a tangi (funeral).

The leaves are used to flavour food and to make tea. The ripe berries can be eaten straight off the tree or kept for use as a seasoning. Drinking kawakawa tea is said to improve kidney function and ease asthma and bronchitis. Kawakawa can also be used as a natural remedy for eczema or dermatitis: the leaves are crushed and mixed with beeswax and olive oil to make an ointment. Chewing on raw kawakawa leaves and berries has a numbing effect, which Māori used to treat toothache.

Those living in the North Island, take a walk around your garden – there's a fair chance you will have some growing there. Failing that, go for a bush walk and you'll find some in no time. You will have to be quick if you want the ripe orange berries, though – birds love them just as much as we do.

KIEKIE
Freycinetia banksii
LOCATED: LOWLAND FORESTS ACROSS AOTEAROA

According to legend, Kiekie (see page 81) and Harakeke were brothers separated as children. Harakeke went to live with Wainui, the mother of waters, and Kiekie stayed with Tāne, god of the forest. Tāne would carry Kiekie on his shoulders wherever they went, which is why we find kiekie clutching to tree trunks high above the forest floor.

Kiekie produces edible flowers and fruit (ureure) that can be harvested in the middle of winter; the flowers have a flavour that is comparable to a fully ripened pear. While they were once a staple food source for Māori, kiekie blossoms are now often consumed by possums before humans get the chance to pick them.

At Hiakai, we process and preserve kiekie blossoms on the day we harvest them, as they tend to deteriorate quickly. Our good friend, expert Māori forager Joe McLeod, let us in on his secret for making kiekie-infused gin. In short, you wash the kiekie, pack them into jars, cover them with gin, set them on a shelf and wait.

At first, when we followed his directions, it seemed nothing was happening. Then, about a month in, I heard a low hissing sound coming from the jars. The once-clear liquid had taken on a pink hue and now had a scent that reminded me of the French liqueur Bénédictine. I called Joe, curious to know if this was normal or if we'd gone wrong somewhere during the preparation process. He assured me that we were on the right track and to leave it for at least another couple of months to 'do its thing'. The end result was a sweet and floral liquor that was ready just in time for summer.

KIOKIO
Blechnum novae-zelandiae
LOCATED: LOWLAND FORESTS ACROSS AOTEAROA

Kiokio is endemic to Aotearoa and belongs to a commonly found family of ferns. It thrives in damp environments, such as riverbanks, swamps and streams.

Traditionally, kiokio fern branches were used to wrap foods being cooked in a hāngi. From late November to February, kiokio produces young fronds that can be found on the tips of the fern leaves.

At Hiakai, we didn't particularly enjoy kiokio fronds to begin with. Kiokio looks very similar to pikopiko; we assumed they could be prepared and eaten in the same way. This was not the case – when eaten

raw, the young fronds are quite bitter and leave an almost soapy aftertaste. It wasn't until we tried simmering them in water that we discovered the fronds release a mild mushroom flavour into the liquid. Even after cooking, the fronds themselves don't make for great eating and are discarded after we've finished extracting as much flavour from them as possible. In this way, we use kiokio fronds to add a mushroom note to stocks, broths, sauces, milks and creams.

KŌKIHI
New Zealand spinach
Tetragonia tetragonioides, Tetragonia implexicoma
LOCATED: COASTAL AREAS ACROSS AOTEAROA

Kōkihi (above left) can usually be found growing abundantly on hillsides close to the beach. The leaves have a crisp texture and taste both refreshing and salty at the same time. Young kōkihi leaves are delicious raw but become more fibrous as they mature. When they reach this stage, they're better suited to sautéing or being blended in purées, soups or even sorbet bases.

In autumn and winter, kōkihi flowers and its small red berries appear. These berries are crunchy, sweet and juicy. I like to collect the berries to garnish raw kaimoana dishes.

Historically, the red juice from the berries was used to make a dye for clothing and writing ink, despite being semi-permanent. When Pākehā arrived and introduced more steadfast dyes, the use of the kōkihi berry declined over time. Captain James Cook and his crew are reported to have used the plant to ward off scurvy; and it has anti-inflammatory properties.

KŌNINI, KŌTUKUTUKU (berries)
Fuchsia excorticata
LOCATED: LOWLAND FORESTS THROUGHOUT AOTEAROA

Of all the native berries of Aotearoa, kōnini are by far my favourite. Small in size, big in flavour, kōnini berries (see page 82, right) are in season from late spring through to mid-summer. Dark red to purplish in colour, they can be eaten straight from the tree. They have a sweet, plum-like taste that was beloved by Māori. Early European settlers also took to them fondly and were soon collecting them to make into jams or add to puddings.

Gathering kōnini berries is not for those with a fear of heights. The best berries are usually found at the top of the tree, which means the forager needs to climb the branches of a tree that is known for its thin, easy-peeling bark. It's a slippery affair – sturdy shoes and a strong grip are needed. I usually attach a small bag to my belt loops so I can always have at least one hand free to grab hold of a branch should the bark send me sliding south.

KOROĪ (kahikatea berries)
Dacrycarpus dacrydioides
LOCATED: ACROSS AOTEAROA

Koroī berries (see page 84, bottom left) grow at the top of the mighty kahikatea tree, which can reach 55 metres in height. Unless you fancy a treacherous climb, the easiest way to gather them is to wait until the berries begin dropping to the forest floor.

The berries are comprised of two bulbous parts fused together. The flesh is red and sweet on one side; the other side is blue, with a flavour similar to black peppercorns. I've found the best way to work with koroī is to split the sides apart. I use the red bulb, either raw or preserved, in sweeter applications, and dehydrate the blue bulb for use in spice mixes.

KOROMIKO, KŌKŌMUKA
Hebe salicifolia, Hebe stricta
LOCATED: ACROSS AOTEAROA

Koromiko (see page 84, top right) was one of the most important herbs of rongoā Māori (Māori medicine). It was used to treat a variety of ailments, such as constipation, ulcers, stomach aches, diarrhoea and dysentery. Dried leaves were sent overseas to New Zealand soldiers during the Second World War to cure the latter.

In the kitchen, koromiko is used more

as an aromatic than as a direct food source. Think of it as you would rosemary or bay leaves – you add them to a braise or roast to enhance flavours. Traditionally, Māori would line hāngi baskets with a generous amount of koromiko to impart a herbaceous depth of flavour to the food. At Hiakai, koromiko is a kitchen staple – we use it to help flavour stocks, soups, hāngi, braises, roasts and teas.

KŪMARA
Sweet potato
Ipomoea batatas
LOCATED: ACROSS AOTEAROA BUT PREDOMINANTLY GROWN IN THE NORTH ISLAND

Kūmara (see page 84, bottom right) is arguably Aotearoa's most recognised and beloved vegetable. It's widely believed that kūmara originated in South America and was brought over to the Pacific region by voyagers who travelled to and settled in Polynesia, before coming to Aotearoa in the 13th century.

Māori were innovative agriculturists and successfully adapted kūmara growing to the much cooler environment in New Zealand. Remains of centuries-old kūmara gardens and pits can be found across Aotearoa, particularly in the northern region of the country where the climate is warmer and kūmara grow more easily.

In modern-day New Zealand, there are many varieties of kūmara, though only three are commercially available: red, or Owairaka Red, has a creamy white flesh; gold, sometimes sold as Toka Toka Gold, has golden skin and flesh, and is sweeter than red; orange kūmara, sometimes sold as Beauregard, has orange flesh and is sweeter than both red and gold. Beauregard can replace yams (sweet potato) in recipes from the United States.

MAMAKU, KŌRAU
Black tree fern
Cyathea medullaris
LOCATED: LOWLAND FORESTS ACROSS AOTEAROA

The mamaku (black tree fern, see page 89) is a striking and popular symbol of Aotearoa. The largest of our tree ferns, it was historically used in the treatment of sunburn, insect bites, blisters, eczema, psoriasis, stomach ulcers and colitis.

Unlike most Māori ingredients, its culinary uses were well documented, despite only being used during times of scarcity, due to its slow reproductive cycle. Mamaku stems were primarily eaten on special occasions, having been cooked in a hāngi or on an open fire.

Mamaku has high levels of collagen, giving the stems a gluey texture, which many early European settlers found disagreeable. However, this substance makes it an ideal substitute for sago.

At Hiakai, we discovered that cooking down mamaku in its juices allowed us to set it as a natural jelly. This discovery led us to create one of our signature petits fours, the Mamaku Pâté de Fruit.

MANONO
Coprosma grandifolia
LOCATED: WIDESPREAD THROUGHOUT AOTEAROA

This tree is quite common in Aotearoa but it still requires a fair amount of effort to trek into the bush to collect its leaves and bark (see page 90).

Traditionally, the leaves were used to make a decoction to treat sores, cuts and bruises. The inner bark was steeped in cold water and placed over body parts suffering aches and pains.

At Hiakai, we collect the leaves and bark and use them to flavour stocks, sauces, dressings and syrups. The bark has a deep golden-orange colour and an earthy flavour with a subtle hint of turmeric; we often add big handfuls of manono leaves to braising liquids or demi-glace. The flavour pairs particularly well with red meat and poultry. Manono leaves are comparable to bay leaves; however, it takes as many as 20 manono leaves to achieve the same level of fragrance that just one or two bay leaves offer.

To help preserve manono between foraging trips, we separate the leaves from the bark and dehydrate whatever we aren't planning to use immediately. Luckily, manono doesn't seem to deteriorate after being dehydrated: it lasts for months in an airtight container if properly dried.

We grind dried manono bark into a fine powder and use it as a seasoning and marinade for kaimoana, meat and vegetables.

MĀNUKA
Tea tree
Leptospermum scoparium
LOCATED: THROUGHOUT AOTEAROA

Mānuka (see page 86) is most often associated with the world-famous honey produced by bees after they collect the highly coveted nectar from its pinkish-white flowers. While honey is its modern claim to fame, there is little evidence to suggest that it had any part to play in the Māori diet. In fact, honeybees weren't introduced to Aotearoa until 1839, when Mary Bumby uplifted two hives from her home in England and set sail toward Hokianga Harbour, where she ultimately settled. However, this is not to say that mānuka had no culinary use at all to Māori.

Mānuka is one of the hottest burning firewoods in the southern hemisphere, making it perfect for heating dense hāngi stones. Mānuka woodsmoke has a punchy yet sweet flavour that pairs well with meat, seafood, root vegetables and, my personal favourite, dark chocolate.

The flowers from mānuka trees have some culinary uses, too. At Hiakai, we pick the flowers, add them to white wine and leave them to infuse for two or three months in the fridge. The result is a refreshing, floral wine that can be served on its own or used as part of a mixed drink.

Mānuka was also used for a wide variety of medicinal purposes. The bark and leaves were boiled down and consumed to relieve stiff joints, inflammation of the breast and constipation. Fresh sap from the mānuka bush was applied to the body to ease bruising and inflammation, and ash from the bark would treat burns and wounds.

MINGIMINGI
Leucopogon fasciculatus
LOCATED: LOWLAND AREAS ACROSS AOTEAROA

There are three different species of mingimingi, which, strangely enough, aren't that closely related. What they do have in common is that they are all small-leafed shrubs that produce small edible berries and all grow in lowland areas across Aotearoa. Māori often used a single, catch-all term for plants that are similar in appearance, which is probably how these three got to be known by the

same name. Mingimingi means 'twisted', perfectly describing the intertwining nature of the branches on all three shrubs.

'Soft' mingimingi and 'tall' mingimingi, as they're colloquially known, produce blue-white berries; 'prickly' mingimingi produces berries that are pinkish-red. There is little recorded information about the traditional culinary uses of mingimingi. Medicinally, it was used to relieve headaches and influenza by boiling the leaves with water and drinking the liquid.

MIRO, TOROMIRO
Brown pine
Prumnopitys ferruginea
LOCATED: THROUGHOUT AOTEAROA

Miro (see page 70, top left), which grows to 25 metres high, can be found throughout Aotearoa, though this native pine is most prevalent on the West Coast of the South Island. Miro can be easily identified by the oval indents on the trunk of the tree, left by flaking bark. Miro gum is highly aromatic and was historically heated and used as an inhalant to treat bronchitis, similar to how we use Vicks VapoRub today.

Miro produces small, edible berries that come into season between late autumn and early winter. These berries, popular with kererū and kākā, are safe to eat but have a large stone in the middle, and an astringent taste that can be quite

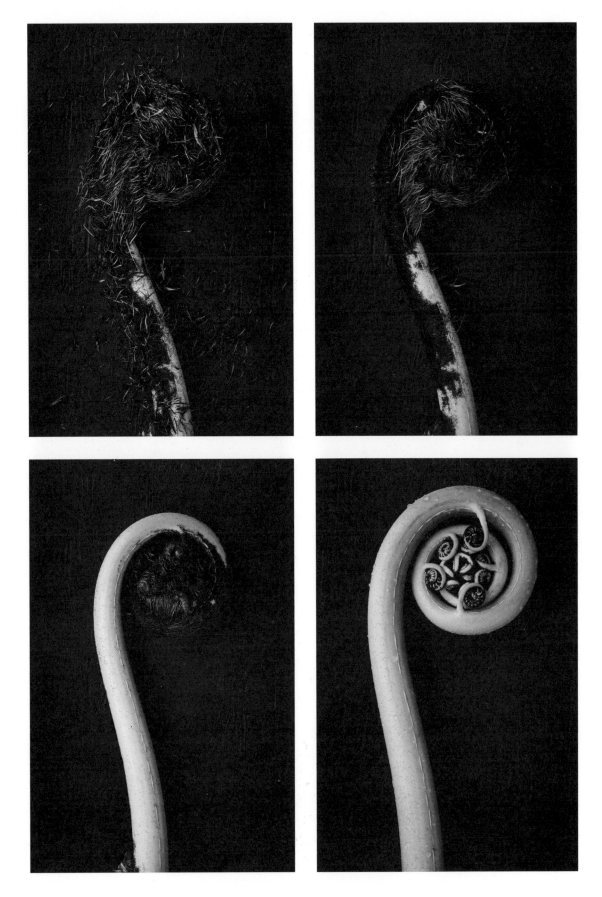

unappealing. At Hiakai, we use small sprigs of miro to make tea. It has a gentle taste of pine and can be consumed as is or used as a base for vinaigrette or fermented drinks.

MŌKEHU
Fern shoots
Pteridium esculentum
LOCATED: ACROSS AOTEAROA

Mōkehu are the young, tender fronds of aruhe (see page 69). Mōkehu has a similar shape to pikopiko and kiokio but is brown in colour and tastes similar to marzipan. This unique flavour makes it ideal to eat raw, or use in desserts instead of almonds.

NĪKAU
Rhopalostylis sapida
LOCATED: COASTAL AND LOWLAND FOREST AREAS

The extremely slow-growing nīkau is native only to Aotearoa and is the southernmost-growing palm in the world. Nīkau thrives in warmer temperatures and is found around coastal and lowland forest areas. Remarkably, it can take almost 200 years for a nīkau palm to become just 10 metres tall.

Nīkau played a key role in traditional Māori life, as a food source, medicine and building material. As a food source, nīkau is best known for the core at the centre of the leaf bud, also known as the palm heart. This is said to be very succulent and have a nutty taste, but removing it kills the entire tree so it was only ever harvested and served on very special occasions. The young shoots of the palm can also be eaten but this must only be done once a year and extreme care must be taken not to injure the tree.

Nīkau produce small, bright red berries once a year. These berries are very hard and not the best eating, but kererū and kākā adore feasting on them between February and November.

Nīkau provided important medicines for early Māori, particularly during childbirth. The sap and pith are said to have laxative properties, helping to relax pelvic muscles. Women drank a decoction made using the sap, during pregnancy and after birth, to relieve pain. The large leaf bases were used to make splints to support broken limbs.

Despite its strong appearance, the nīkau has faced hard times in recent decades. It's a delicate tree that needs to be handled with care and respect. In some areas of Aotearoa, nīkau is listed as endangered and special reserves have been set up in order to help restore numbers. I personally haven't eaten nīkau palm for these reasons and I wouldn't encourage anyone to do so. Conserving plants and animals for future generations is far more important than culinary pursuits.

PIKOPIKO
Fern shoots
Asplenium bulbiferum (hen and chicken
fern), ***Polystichum richardii*** (common
shield fern)
LOCATED: LOWLAND FORESTS
THROUGHOUT AOTEAROA

Pikopiko (see page 93) are the young,
curled shoots of ferns. They prefer to grow
in damp, sheltered areas. The best time
for picking is during autumn and winter,
when the moisture content of the soil is at
its highest and sunlight hours are shortest.
Gathering pikopiko can be difficult,
however, as the shoots are often hidden
among dense foliage on the forest floor.

Pikopiko was one of the foods eaten
at Matariki feasts. Once harvested, it
can be peeled and washed to remove
the bitterness, then steamed, boiled or
stir-fried, or simply used as an attractive
garnish.

Raw pikopiko has a crunchy texture,
and a pleasant, slightly bitter aftertaste.
Pikopiko also tastes great sautéed in a
little oil and salt. At Hiakai, we prefer to
preserve pikopiko by brining or pickling
it, to cut through some of the natural
bitterness.

PŪHĀ, RAURIKI
Sow thistle
Sonchus oleraceus
LOCATED: GROWS WILD THROUGHOUT
AOTEAROA

Pūhā (see page 94, right), a member of
the sow thistle family, is a leafy green that
grows easily in most parts of the country.
Left to its own devices, it will quickly
become a pest and overrun most gardens.
It's for this reason that commercial pūhā
production hasn't taken off here, despite
its widespread use. Still, at most New
Zealand farmers' markets, there's a good
chance that one or two vendors will be
selling pūhā by the bunch.

Pūhā has a lot going for it. It's high
in vitamin C, contains magnesium, iron,
potassium and calcium, and provides
fibre and protein. As a medicine, it's said
to work as a digestive tonic and blood
purifier. The leaves are most commonly
used for both food and medicine. The
stems contain a milky sap that can be used
to make a natural chewing gum. This is
done by cutting through several stems of
pūhā to let the sap seep out and begin to
dry. Once it's dry enough to handle, the
various pieces of sap can be formed into
a single bite-sized piece of chewing gum.
This technique was common practice
among Māori and early European settlers
as a way to treat toothache, bad breath
and gum disease.

Pūhā has a bitter flavour, which makes it better suited to braising, pickling or fermenting. I wasn't a big fan of it as a child but as my palate has matured, I've developed a fondness for the punchy, mustard-like taste that this 'pest' green provides. It has a numbing effect on the throat and tongue when served raw, so it's best to avoid putting it in a salad, or to give it a quick sauté. Pūhā's bitterness can be tamed and its flavour improved by bruising the leaves during the preparation process. To do this, firmly rub handfuls of pūhā between your hands as you're cleaning it under running water. The leaves will wilt and the green colour will deepen. After all of the pūhā has been bruised, it's ready to use as you please.

RANGIORA
Brachyglottis repanda
LOCATED: ACROSS THE NORTH ISLAND, TOP OF THE SOUTH ISLAND

Rangiora (above left) is a small shrub, growing to about 5 to 7 metres in height. Its leaves were traditionally bruised, mashed and mixed with oil to treat wounds and sores. The leaves are large and robust, and are ideal for wrapping food during cooking. At Hiakai, we often wrap meat, fish or pudding batter in rangiora leaves and place them into a steamer, hāngi or oven to cook, which infuses a gentle olive aroma to the food.

Rangiora contains a very small amount of an alkaloid poison, so it should be used only for wrapping food, then discarded.

RED MATIPO
Myrsine australis
LOCATED: LOWLAND SHRUB AND
COASTAL FORESTS THROUGHOUT
AOTEAROA

Red matipo (see page 96) is a hardy shrub found only in Aotearoa. It can survive almost any weather condition and grows up to 6 metres in height. Traditionally, red matipo leaves were boiled into tea and used to treat toothache. Māori also used them to relieve arthritic complaints, as a remedy for various skin problems and intestinal worms, and as a general tonic.

We didn't think this plant offered us much in the restaurant to begin with. Despite a mild apple flavour, the crisp raw leaves are more or less inedible, and the branches bear no fruit. Initial research into the plant yielded zero results for historical culinary use.

It wasn't until we needed to create a dish with a background note of apple that red matipo reappeared in our kitchen. We sought to extract the flavour by steeping bundles of fresh branches into a light simple syrup. We left the infusion to sit for a week and, when we checked on it, the syrup had become gelatinous, with the light apple flavour we were seeking. So far we've created red matipo sorbets, ice creams, curds, vinegars and kombuchas.

TAEWA, RĪWAI
Māori potato
Solanum tuberosum
LOCATED: THROUGHOUT AOTEAROA
BUT PREDOMINANTLY GROWN IN THE
NORTH ISLAND

Taewa (see page 98, bottom right) is the umbrella term for the many varieties of potatoes cultivated by Māori, including urenika, moemoe, huakaroro, raupī and karuparera, which have been grown in Aotearoa for hundreds of years. They are both a staple crop and a taonga. By the 1800s, taewa had also become an important crop to be harvested and on-sold, helping introduce Māori to European economics.

Taewa produce fewer tubers than introduced varieties of potatoes. This means they're not suited to meeting the demands of modern supermarkets and are not often seen for sale outside farmers' markets. However, that's not to say there's no market for them. Consumers, particularly in the restaurant industry, have shown growing interest in working with heritage breeds of taewa and farmers are starting to produce larger quantities to meet demand. If you can manage to track taewa down, they boil and steam well and have a sweet, nutty flavour and smooth texture. The skin is quite tender so peeling them is unnecessary.

At Hiakai, we regularly feature different varieties of taewa on our menu

throughout the year. We work closely with our growers, who plant specific varieties for us to use.

TARATA

Lemonwood

Pittosporum eugenioides

LOCATED: LOWLAND AND SUB-ALPINE FORESTS THROUGHOUT AOTEAROA

Tarata (see page 84, top left) is a native evergreen that releases a citrus fragrance when the leaves are crushed together. Early Māori collected tarata flowers and leaves and mixed them with fats to create ointments and perfumes. They would also collect and chew the tree gum as a remedy for bad breath.

Tarata is a staple in the Hiakai pantry. We collect large quantities of leaves on a weekly basis to be used in a multitude of ways. Though the leaves have a similar scent to lemon verbena, tarata leaves are much tougher and unsuitable for eating straight from the tree. However, the lemony fragrance and flavour can be obtained by steeping the leaves into syrups and vinegar infusions. We also dehydrate and grind the leaves into a powder that we use to add a subtle citrus note to anything from fish to desserts. It's worth noting that the dehydration process does tend to dull the brightness of the fresh leaves.

At the restaurant, to turn tarata into a powder without losing any of the bright colour, we pour liquid nitrogen over a bundle of leaves, then shatter them into a powder than can be used immediately or stored in the freezer. Don't try this at home, though – it's tricky even for professionals.

Tarata flowers bloom between October and December and are highly fragrant. These are also a prized ingredient for us at the restaurant. When the flowers are in season, we concentrate our foraging efforts on collecting as many as we can. Once harvested, we prepare them similarly to the leaves, but because the flowers are more robust they hold themselves well in ferments. This extra potency from the flowers makes them ideal to steep into alcohol, ferment into kombucha or brew into our personal favourite, tarata 'champagne'.

TARO

Colocasia esculenta

LOCATED: UPPER NORTH ISLAND

There's some debate about whether taro (see page 98, top left and right) was a significant food source for Māori. Many believe that it was brought to New Zealand by early Polynesian settlers and thrived in warmer parts of the country. Others believe that it failed to grow in Aotearoa's largely cool climate. However, taro does feature in accounts from early European settlers of the gardens and food

they observed here. Carbon-dating also reveals taro deposits dating back to the 14th century, so it seems highly likely that taro was commonly grown and eaten in some northern regions.

Taro roots and leaves are edible, but both are poisonous when raw and need to be thoroughly cooked before being eaten. Taro root is very starchy and was traditionally cooked in a hāngi along with other root vegetables. Because taro is difficult to grow, it was only eaten on special occasions and was thought of as kai rangatira (food for important people).

Thanks to my combined Māori and Sāmoan heritage, taro featured on our table more often than potatoes. My grandmother would simply peel the taro then cook it low and slow in coconut cream with onions and garlic. The entire house would take on the aroma, even making its way to the backyard where we'd be playing. With the taro leaves, she'd make creamed lūʻau, a Sāmoan delicacy. Lūʻau is made by baking the leaves in coconut cream until completely soft. The result is similar to creamed spinach but richer and with more depth.

We've done a fair bit of cooking taro in a hāngi at Hiakai, but our favourite way to prepare it is to make Taro Gratin (see page 192). This was inspired by the Sunday mornings I spent cooking taro with my grandmother – all the ingredients are the same, we just use slightly fancier tools and techniques to relive the memory.

TAWA
Beilschmiedia tawa
LOCATED: LOWLAND FORESTS IN THE NORTH ISLAND AND SOUTH-EAST SOUTH ISLAND

There are a number of Māori proverbs about tawa trees and the berries they produce. My favourite compares the chit-chat of children playing to the crackle and pop of tawa berries cooking on an open fire: *Ko te ahi tawa hai whakarite* – They are as noisy as a tawa fire. As an aunt of four young nieces and two nephews, who are a boisterous force to be reckoned with when together, I can easily see how this light-hearted proverb came to be.

There are three edible parts to the tawa tree: bark, berry flesh and berry kernels. Water infused with tawa bark creates a naturally sweet drink that was highly enjoyed by Māori and early European settlers. While tawa berries can be eaten straight from the tree, they taste strongly of turpentine and were only really eaten when nothing better could be found. The real treasure was the tawa berry kernels, one of the most prized foods of the Māori diet.

Traditionally, tawa berries were collected in large quantities, then placed into a woven basket and set in a stream, so that the flesh could be removed easily. The kernels were then put in a hāngi and cooked for a full day (sometimes two) to soften them. Once fully cooked, the kernels were dried again to preserve them for later use. When the time came to eat the kernels, they were boiled and pounded into a meal-like mixture, similar to grits or porridge. Another method was to roast the kernels on an open fire, causing them to explode and pop.

TĪ KŌUKA (shoots)
Cabbage tree
Cordyline australis
LOCATED: ACROSS AOTEAROA

Tī kōuka trees (see page 101), which look a little like palm trees, can be found standing tall and proud in even the most humble New Zealand gardens. The sight of these native beauties can evoke an immediate sense of relaxation.

Tī kōuka (see page 98, bottom left) had many medicinal uses. Juice was extracted from the leaves and applied to cuts, grazes and sores. Leaves were boiled to make tea, which helped ease diarrhoea and stomach pains, while the young shoots were given to nursing mothers and to children suffering from colic.

Few people realise that tī kōuka was once a staple food source of Aotearoa. Climb to the top of a tī kōuka tree, place your hand in the middle of the leaves and you'll feel a thick shoot. This is the young tī kōuka shoot and it's delicious, whether eaten raw or cooked. The flavour is similar to cabbage, which is why it came to be more commonly known as the cabbage tree to non-Māori.

Tī kōuka was a source of sugar for early Māori. The roots were dug up, cooked and ground to a pulp to release the natural sugars inside. Early Europeans even managed to make alcohol from the plant, which whalers and sealers drank when all other options ran out.

Spring sees the arrival of young tī kōuka flowers, which are also an excellent food source. The stems are best enjoyed raw and have a slight nutty taste, similar to green almond. The flower buds have an entirely different flavour profile: they are mildly bitter with a slight cumin undertone. When dehydrated, they taste like a distant relative of aniseed.

WHENUA: LAND

HUHU GRUBS
Prionoplus reticularis
LOCATED: ACROSS AOTEAROA

Dig down into the damp cavities of rotten logs and you'll often find one of Aotearoa's finest delicacies – the huhu grub (see page 102). These fat, wrinkly bugs (larvae of the endemic huhu beetle) provided a rich source of fat to the early Māori diet. Considered one of nature's greatest little recyclers, huhu grubs munch through decomposed trees that would otherwise bury the forest floor.

Today, most people approach eating huhu grubs with a 'fear factor' mentality. But while they'll never win an award for being the most attractive morsel on the planet, huhu grubs taste great and no serious foodie should be afraid to give them a go.

To enjoy a huhu grub: first grab your axe. Split a decaying log right down the middle, then pluck out a grub and eat it raw. As you bite down, a small burst of peanut butteriness will pop in your mouth. If you prefer a less 'lively' version, sauté the grubs with a little garlic and salt. The

grub's outer shell expands and becomes crisp when cooked in a pan of hot oil, adding a delicious crunch.

KĀKĀ
Bush parrot
Nestor meridionalis
LOCATED: ISLAND AND COASTAL AREAS; NEAR PREDATOR-CONTROLLED AREAS

The kākā is a large, forest-dwelling parrot known for being playful and talkative. Māori often make reference to the kākā's chatty characteristics when describing people: someone known for being a gasbag is often described as *he kākā waha nui* (a big-mouthed kākā). Kākā are greedy as well as gregarious – they eat a varied diet of native berries, seeds, insects, nectar and sap, often until they're too full to fly.

Kākā were one of the few birds that Māori kept as pets, often teaching them to mimic other species and using them as decoys when hunting. This didn't stop them from becoming food themselves – kākā were a staple of the Māori diet, and European settlers also took to eating them in great numbers. Today, there are fewer than 10,000 kākā left in Aotearoa. Hunting and eating them is no longer legal.

KERERŪ
Wood pigeon
Hemiphaga novaeseelandiae
LOCATED: ACROSS AOTEAROA

Kererū, Aotearoa's only endemic pigeon, is the last remaining native bird capable of swallowing large fruit. They can be spotted throughout Aotearoa but are most abundant in Northland, Nelson and the West Coast of the South Island. Kererū are prolific seed dispersers, an essential skill required to help keep our native forests thriving for generations to come. The distinctive noisy beating of their wings signals their presence to anyone enjoying New Zealand's forests.

Kererū, also known as kūkupa, were an important food for Māori. Though the birds aren't considered threatened, hunting them has been illegal since 1922. This has been a source of tension between Māori and conservationists. The Treaty of Waitangi, signed in 1840, guaranteed Māori the right to hunt kererū as food. The removal of this right is still hotly debated almost 100 years after the ban was first put in place.

KIORE
Polynesian rat
Rattus exulans
LOCATED: ACROSS AOTEAROA

Longstanding wisdom had kiore being brought to Aotearoa by Polynesian explorers in the 13th century. Traditionally, kiore were hunted and skinned before being cooked in a hāngi or over an open fire. The rats were a rich source of fat and protein for Māori. The meat was packed into calabashes and covered in rendered fat, while the skins were kept to weave into cloaks. Kiore huahua (preserved kiore) was considered a treat that was reserved for special occasions, and sometimes exchanged as a form of currency between iwi. After huge eradication efforts, kiore were thought to be extinct by the 1920s. Luckily, a small number survived and today the kiore population is thriving again. It may be the only rat species in existence that has had two offshore island sanctuaries set up to protect its numbers.

KIWI
Apteryx
LOCATED: ACROSS AOTEAROA

The kiwi – te manu huna a Tāne (the hidden bird of Tāne) – is Aotearoa's national icon. The endemic, flightless, nocturnal bird is a taonga to Māori, who have long held strong cultural and spiritual connections to it.

Traditionally, kiwi were used for both food and cloak-making. The meat was considered a delicacy that was only to be eaten by chiefs because of its taonga status. The cooked birds were commonly preserved by being covered in rendered fat and stored away in the pātaka for future consumption. Kiwi skins and soft feathers were used to make kahu kiwi (kiwi feather cloaks woven for those of high rank and worn during important ceremonies, such as weddings, tangi or the birth of a chief's child).

Unfortunately, the kiwi is at high risk of becoming extinct during our lifetime. The introduction of predators such as possums and stoats, combined with habitat loss from deforestation and the environmental impacts of a growing human population, have had devastating effects on kiwi numbers. There are currently fewer than 68,000 left, across five species: North Island brown, rowi, tokoeka, little spotted and great spotted.

Hunting or eating kiwi is now illegal; anyone who is caught doing so can be fined up to $100,000 or face up to two years' imprisonment.

I haven't personally eaten kiwi but, from the few recorded accounts of the bird's flavour, I'm not sure that I want to. Charles Douglas, a 19th-century explorer, described the taste as 'a piece of pork boiling in an old coffin'. As a chef, I believe the flavour of food is dependent on the skill of the cook – maybe Mr Douglas lacked much knowledge of the culinary arts. Even so, I'm quite content with the flavour of kiwi remaining a great unknown. Conserving our national bird is far more important than curious consumption.

TĪTĪ
Muttonbird, sooty shearwater
Puffinus griseus
LOCATED: TĪTĪ ISLANDS

Tītī (see pages 106–7) are prized seabirds, harvested between April and May. Each year, groups of people belonging to Rakiura (Stewart Island) Māori travel to the 36 islands around the southern tip of New Zealand, where they exercise their ancestral hunting rights. No one outside of Rakiura Māori is allowed to set foot on any of the Tītī Islands – the only way for non-Rakiura Māori to gain access is by marriage.

Tītī are comparable to duck in terms of size and fat percentage, with a complex

flavour that's a cross between anchovy and game. Traditionally, the cooked birds were covered in rendered fat then packed in pōhā tītī (kelp bags) to preserve them (see page 62). Nowadays, it's more common for the birds to be cured in large amounts of salt and sealed in buckets that can be more easily shipped across Aotearoa for sale. The salted birds develop a funky smell over time, which only seems to amplify when cooked. Some find this odour off-putting while others love it.

At Hiakai, we are lucky to have a few suppliers who send us unsalted birds that don't give off the same aroma as their salted counterparts. Getting unsalted tītī to the mainland is a tricky business. The majority of the Tītī Islands have little to no electricity, let alone fridges. There are a few hunters with boats that boast refrigeration but these are rare. In any case, space is at a premium and they might be docked for several days at time before heading back to the mainland.

To keep unsalted birds in optimal condition between trips, the hunters leave them encased in the plucking wax they'd usually remove before salting. Leaving the wax on helps prevents 'nasties' getting in and stops the skin from drying out in the fridge.

Since the hunting season is so short, we have to order a year's supply in a single hit. Once our waxed birds make it to mainland shores, they're shipped to the restaurant where we store them in

our freezers. My favourite way to prepare fresh tītī is to confit them but, if time and bird stocks allow, we also cook them slowly in our woodfire oven, Peking duck-style.

TŪĪ
Prosthemadera novaeseelandiae
LOCATED: ACROSS AOTEAROA

Tūī are widespread throughout Aotearoa and enjoy strong population numbers. Blessed with a dual voice box, tūī are famed for their singing ability and can mimic human speech. They are boisterous and charismatic, often seen swooping from sky to forest then back again in an attempt to find a mate.

Māori kept tūī as pets as well as for food. Traditionally, the birds were cooked and stored in calabashes, covered with their own rendered fat. These pots were often decorated with the bird's feathers, then presented as centrepieces at large feasts. European settlers also hunted tūī, preferring to eat them in pies. Tūī were the first of New Zealand's native birds to become legally protected, when hunting them was outlawed in 1873.

Introduced pests such as possums, stoats and rats remain a threat to tūī and their eggs, but the birds have also benefited from the introduction of various European flowers and fruiting plants.

WEKA
Gallirallus australis
LOCATED: ACROSS AOTEAROA

The flightless weka (see page 109) is well known for its cheeky and curious nature. Māori found many uses for the endemic bird beyond eating. Weka feathers were woven into kahu weka (weka feather cloaks) that were only woven for people of high rank; there are several on display at Te Papa Tongarewa. Weka oil, usually infused with crushed tarata leaves, was commonly used to make fragrances.

Weka are now on the threatened species list. The birds are fully protected on mainland Aotearoa – hunting them is only allowed by permit on some islands off Rakiura Stewart Island and Rēkohu Chatham Islands.

I was lucky enough to try weka via friends living on the Chatham Islands. When the box of frozen birds arrived, I was expecting something similar to duck. Instead, the skin was as rubbery as pigskin with a thick layer of yellowy-white fat beneath the rind. The birds weren't as plump as ducks but the flesh did share the same reddish-brown tinge.

I decided to go with my initial instincts and make weka confit. Reactions were mixed when I posted my progress on social media: some were intrigued and enlightened, others expressed outrage that I was about to eat one of Aotearoa's most beloved birds. When the moment came to try the finished product, the result was abysmal. Despite cooking it low and slow for several hours in a mixture of weka fat and duck fat, the skin had tightened like plastic and the flesh was stringy and dry.

I went back to the drawing board. The skin was the biggest problem, because it didn't allow any moisture to penetrate the meat despite being meticulously scored. I removed the skin entirely, doing my best not to disturb the layer of fat directly beneath. I heated a small cast-iron pot and gathered all the usual ingredients for a braise – mirepoix, stock, wine, bouquet garni – and began round two of my weka experiment. This time, I tasted success. The meat fell off the bone and the braising liquid had taken on the gaminess of the bird.

EXTINCT ANIMALS

KOREKE
New Zealand quail
Coturnix novaezelandiae

Koreke was the only type of quail endemic to Aotearoa. They were abundant throughout the country and preferred to live in grassy shrubland areas.

For centuries, Māori hunted koreke

extensively, both to eat and to use the feathers for clothing. The arrival of European settlers signalled the beginning of the end for the birds, however. Their habitat disappeared when land was cleared to make way for the growing population and koreke couldn't evade the increased number of hunters. Some accounts claim that European hunters could kill between 20 and 40 birds each a day. This level of hunting was unsustainable and koreke were presumed extinct by 1875.

KURĪ
Polynesian dog
Canis lupus familiaris

Kurī were a breed of Polynesian dog that came to Aotearoa during the great migration from the Pacific Islands in the 13th century. Māori had a great affection for kurī, keeping them as pets and training them to be trusty hunting assistants. Instead of barking like European dogs, kurī let out long, sorrowful howls.

Kurī were also a highly valued food source that provided much-needed protein to the Māori diet. Captain Cook reported that kurī meat tasted 'as good as lamb'. Māori also turned the skins into kahu kurī (dogskin cloaks) and turned the bones and teeth into jewellery and fish hooks.

By the 1860s, kurī had disappeared. It's unclear exactly how they became extinct. Many believe they slowly died out as a result of interbreeding with European dogs. Others think it was caused by the change in diet, or the post-colonisation practice of shooting wild crossbreeds on sight. The last remaining kurī and her pup were taxidermied and can be seen in the Land Mammals Collection at Te Papa Tongarewa.

MOA

Moa inhabited Aotearoa long before Māori arrived. Some species of moa towered over other native birds, reaching more than three metres tall with necks outstretched. The flightless birds, which are related to the kiwi, were one of the largest bird species to have roamed the earth. Until Māori arrived, the moa's only predator was the pouakai (Haast's eagle).

The nine species of slow-moving moa were easy prey for Māori, who ate their flesh, turned their skins and feathers into clothing and carved their bones into fish hooks and jewellery. Less than 200 years after Māori arrived in Aotearoa, they had hunted moa into extinction. The Haast's eagle, which had relied heavily on moa as a food source, also became extinct as a result.

KAIMOANA: SEAFOOD

Aotearoa's network of streams, rivers, lakes and coastlines are home to 80 per cent of the country's total biodiversity. There are approximately 1000 species of marine fish, 58 species of freshwater fish, 2000 species of molluscs, 400 species of echinoderms (things such as sea cucumbers and sea urchins) and 900 species of seaweed residing in our waters.

Not all these plants and creatures are edible. Not all of those that are edible were eaten by Māori or are endemic. But kaimoana was the most important and abundant source of protein for Māori. This section gives an overview of the types of kaimoana that were traditionally eaten, the importance they hold for Māori, the role they played in early relations between Māori and Pākehā, and the status of these taonga today.

IKA TAKUTAI
Fish

Aotearoa has over 15,000 kilometres of coastline, surrounded by the Pacific Ocean and Tasman Sea. Māori have a deep spiritual connection with the sea, and fishing is an activity steeped in protocol and tradition. It is a sacred ritual, and respect for Tangaroa, god of the sea, is to be observed at all times. A karakia seeking protection and an abundance of kaimoana is customary before commencing fishing and the first fish caught is to be returned to the sea to give thanks to Tangaroa.

While there are numerous well-documented accounts of fishing methods and activities, there is limited detail about the full spectrum of fish that were consumed, though Māori oral history and archeological study of early Māori middens provide some insight into the types of species sought. Of the hundreds of species that reside in our coastal waters, those below represent the species for which there is unrefuted evidence of them being a part of the early Māori diet.

Araara
Trevally
Pseudocaranx dentex
Trevally, with its light blue-grey top and silver-white underside, is a hugely popular fish in New Zealand, found around the top of the North Island, where the water temperatures are warmer. Its flesh makes for great eating, especially when smoked, marinated or raw, as sashimi.

Aua, Makawhiti
Yellow-eyed mullet
Aldrichetta forsteri
A slight fish, with its grey-green top and white underside, and weighing in at under half a kilogram, the yellow-eyed mullet is nowadays found throughout Aotearoa's inland coastal waters, with the exception of Fiordland. More often than not, it's used as bait.

Hāpuku
Groper
Polyprion oxygeneios
Hāpuku is a large, slow-growing fish that averages around 6–8 kilograms in weight but can grow up to an impressive 80 kilograms. It's found in waters right around Aotearoa. It has firm, lean, white flesh with very few bones and remains moist with heavy flakes when cooked – perfect for steaks and smoking. Hāpuku also produces delicious roe.

Hauture
Jack mackerel
Trachurus declivis, T. novaezelandiae, T. murphyi
Hauture belong to the same family as trevally, kōheru and yellowtail kingfish. They can be distinguished from kōheru by their lateral line, which has a distinct kink midway down the side of the body. They can be found all around Aotearoa but are most abundant along the west coast of the North Island.

Slender jack mackerel (*T. murphyi*) is a large, long-bodied, blue-green species. It was first discovered in Aotearoa in the early 1980s and its territory extends from the eastern Pacific Ocean to the southern.

Hauture has oily flesh and is suited to most cooking methods.

Hoka
Red cod
Pseudophycis bachus, P. barbata, P. breviuscula
Hoka, or red cod, is most commonly found in the Canterbury and Westland regions. With an average weight of 0.8–1.3 kilograms, hoka has a distinctive pinkish-grey colour that changes to red when the fish dies.

It has a barbel – a protruding fleshy filament – on its lower jaw, which it can use to detect prey buried in mud or sand.

Hoka is great for smoking, frying, baking or poaching.

Hoki
Blue hake, New Zealand whiptail, blue grenadier
Macruronus novaezelandiae

Hoki is Aotearoa's most important commercial fish species – annually contributing $185 million to the local economy. It is most abundant in the upper South Island, found between 300 and 600 metres deep.

In 2010, Greenpeace International added hoki to its seafood 'red list' and Forest and Bird gives hoki an E grade. Both organisations claim major damage to the sea floor due to trawling and incidental 'bycatch' of other species, such as fur seals, albatrosses, petrels and sharks.

Ihe
Piper, garfish
Hyporhamphus ihi

Piper or garfish are endemic to Aotearoa, distributed throughout the country in shallow inshore waters. It's a long, slender fish with a pointed beak.

They were an important source of food and bait for early Māori, and an item of great cultural significance. They were traditionally caught using finely woven harakeke nets that were dragged across seagrass beds in shallow harbours.

A seine-like technique was usually employed, in which one end of the net was fixed to the shore and the other end was dragged out and around in a large arc, then pulled back to shore. The same technique is still used by some modern fishers.

Kahawai
Arripis trutta

The mighty kahawai (see page 116) is Aotearoa's second-most commonly caught fish. The name kahawai translates to 'brave' or 'strong' (kaha) 'water' (wai), which refers to the fish's tendency to jump and fight when caught.

Kahawai was an important food item for Māori, especially in the East Cape. Māori used to fish for kahawai with flax nets, sometimes up to 2 kilometres in length, or with lures that had shiny pāua inserts. Māori at the Motu River used to bury the fish for up to a year to preserve them.

Kahawai are found predominantly around the lower North Island and top half of the South Island, particularly around Kaikōura and Cook Strait. They are silver-coloured with a greenish-blue tinge, weighing on average at 2–5 kilograms.

With its firm texture and oily flesh, it is popular as a smoked fish but can also be baked, marinated, poached, fried or put into a curry.

Kōheru
Decapterus koheru

Kōheru is endemic to New Zealand and can be fished from the Three Kings Islands to the southern North Island. Normally weighing around 0.5–1 kilogram, it's closely related to the hauture or jack mackerel.

Koinga, Kāraerae
Spiny shark
Squalus acanthias

Koinga was a highly consumed food source for Māori. As well as being cooked and eaten fresh, its liver oil was used for as a base for paint; teeth and bones were used for fish hooks and jewellery.

It weighs in at around 3.5–4.5 kilograms, has distinctive white spots along its side, and these days is most commonly eaten as fish and chips.

Kumukumu, Pūwhaiau
Red gurnard
Chelidonichthys kumu

The ever-popular red gurnard (see page 119) is found throughout Aotearoa, except for the southern points of the South Island.

It has a beautiful reddish-orange top side and pectoral fins which spread open like butterfly wings, as a display or to startle potential predators.

Gurnard can also make sounds using 'drumming' muscles that are beaten against a gas bladder. Their common English name comes from the old French word 'gornard', meaning 'grunter' or 'to grunt'.

Kuparu
John Dory
Zeus faber

Kuparu, or John Dory, are caught year-round in the coastal waters off northern Aotearoa, most commonly from Bay of Plenty north. It's in fact most abundant along the inshore coasts of the Bay of Plenty.

John Dory are oval-shaped with no scales and are distinguished by a dark-blue spot ringed with white on each side of their body.

Pickled kuparu was gifted to Captain James Cook during his first voyage to Aotearoa in 1769.

Makohuarau, Tupere
School shark, grey shark, flake
Galeorhinus galeus

A medium-sized shark, on average weighing 5–15 kilograms, the makohuarau has a white underside, grey top and an elongated snout. They grow up to 2 metres in length. As with most sharks eaten in Aotearoa, they're popularly served in fish and chip shops.

Makorepe
Elephant fish
Callorhinchus milii

The makorepe is found only in Aotearoa, most commonly along the east coast of the South Island.

Silver-bronze, with scaleless skin and a large, brown, irregular-shaped spot, it's notable for a long trunk-like snout. Makorepe usually weigh 3–4 kilograms and are closely related to sharks and stingrays.

Mangā
Barracuda, Cook Strait sailfish
Thyrsites atun

Mangā are most abundantly fished in Cook Strait, the Marlborough Sounds and the Kaikōura Coast, and normally weigh 1.5–3 kilograms.

Traditionally, Māori would preserve the flesh of the fish by hanging it in the sun to dry.

Noted for their oily flesh and for having lots of large bones (and sharp teeth!), they are best grilled, fried or smoked.

Mangō, Makō
Rig shark, lemonfish, spotted dogfish
Mustelus lenticulatus

Mangō are found throughout Aotearoa but most prefer shallow bays during spring and summer. They usually weigh 3–4 kilograms and have greyish-bronze

skin and white spots.

Early Māori often dried mangō meat to eat later, and used their skin for sandpaper. Today, mangō is commonly served as fish and chips.

Mararī
Butterfish, greenbone
Odax pullus

Mararī, or butterfish, is an endemic species of kelpfish found in the shallow waters around Aotearoa's coast. It's a surface-dwelling fish, not often found swimming below 15 metres.

Mararī begin life and mature as females before changing into males when they reach approximately 35–40 centimetres in length.

With a distinctive cylindrical, elongated shape, butterfish are dark blue to dark black in colour, and are sometimes called greenbone owing to the green tinge of their bones.

Butterfish are valued for their clean, delicate flavour, translucent flesh and ability to flake well. They're beautifully tender and moist when cooked, hence the 'butteriness' they are attributed with.

Matiri
Bluenose
Hyperoglyphe antarctica

Bluenose is a long-lived, slow-growing relative of warehou. It's widespread

throughout the lower reaches of Aotearoa's oceans. This deep-water habitat has forced them to adapt to the environment, which has resulted in a rich 'antifreeze' existing in the fish's muscle structure. This type of fat is found in many of the world's most popular fish, such as king salmon, northern halibut, butterfish and black cod.

In Aotearoa, bluenose have a blue-grey/silver colouring and large eyes, and weigh in at 5–6 kilograms.

The flesh of bluenose has medium to thick, moist flakes and can be cooked in a variety of ways: baked, on the barbecue, poached, fried or in soups and chowder.

Mauhauaitu
Grey mullet
Mugil cephalus

Grey mullet inhabits both marine and freshwater, and is most abundant in the North Island along inshore coastal waters.

It is a small fish with grey-silver colouring, and distinctive blue-green stripes.

The fish is excellent smoked but can also be baked, cooked in a casserole, poached or steamed. The roe of grey mullet is considered a delicacy.

Moki
Blue moki
Latridopsis ciliaris

Despite the similarities in their common names, blue moki is not closely related to red moki, the latter being a species of morwong. Blue moki belongs to the trumpeter family and can be fished all around Aotearoa.

A decent-sized fish, normally weighing 3–5 kilograms, blue moki is blue-grey in colour, sometimes with one or two brown-bronze blotches, large scales and large lips.

Curiously, blue moki feed on a range of crabs, shellfish and worms, which they suck up from the sandy or muddy seafloor. They otherwise eat small fish and seaweed, and live around rocky reefs at all depths accessible by a freediver.

Māori think of blue moki as having special significance. They are thought to spawn at Cape Runaway – traditional fishing grounds for blue moki and where customary fishing took place in earlier times. Local iwi consider fishing blue moki by set nets in this area to be culturally offensive.

Pātiki
Sand flounder, yellowbelly flounder
Rhombosolea plebeia

The diminutive pātiki is only found in Aotearoa; it is most abundant along the coast of Tasman Bay and the east coast of the South Island. They are a flatfish and have a dark olive top side and white-yellow underside.

Traditionally, Māori caught pātiki by fishing at night, along mudflats and using wooden spears. They would attract them using light from a torch made of pine, spearing them with ease.

Pātiki is best baked, grilled, barbecued or fried. The flesh will flake easily when cooked.

Pōrae
Trumpeter
Nemadactylus douglasii
Pōrae is sometimes described as snapper's poor cousin. The pōrae is in fact from the same family as tarakihi but is distinguished by its colouring, lack of a dark shoulder band and more pronounced lips.

Silver-toned and with a blue-green tinge, pōrae are most abundant along the northeast coast of the North Island. They usually weigh 2–4 kilograms.

They are fast-growing, capable of growing up to 28 centimetres in a single year when young. Despite this they are quite long-lived – large fish may be up to 30 years old.

Pūwhara
Monkfish, stargazer
Kathetostoma giganteum
Pūwhara are most commonly found at the southern tip of the South Island.

Weighing 1.5–5 kilograms, they are scaleless, with brownish-grey skin and multiple spots, and a prominent head with upward-looking eyes.

Their appearance can be offputting to some but the flesh is nonetheless well suited to baking, barbecuing, poaching, frying, steaming or using in soups and chowders.

Rāwaru, Pākirikiri
Blue cod
Parapercis colias
Endemic to Aotearoa, blue cod (see page 120) are the third most popular recreational fish here and are an iconic South Island species.

Traditionally, Māori gave the heads of rāwaru back to the sea as offerings to the god Maru before they returned from fishing.

Male rāwaru are blue with greenish colouring; females have similar colouring but are mottled. Interestingly, they can change sex from female to male, and males are generally larger than females.

Divers often find they can approach blue cod quite easily. An inquisitive fish, they will also sometimes approach divers and nip their fingers, and even their ears.

Tāmure
Snapper
Pagrus auratus
Despite its English name, snapper (see page 123) is a member of the sea bream family, and is Aotearoa's most popular fish for both commercial and recreational fishers. It can be found all over the country but is most abundant along the east and west coast of the North Island.

All snapper begin life as females; then, at three or four years of age, approximately half change sex, balancing the adult population evenly between male and female. They can live a long time – the oldest recorded specimen was 63 years old.

Snapper's average weight ranges between 2 and 10 kilograms, and they make for versatile cooking: you can poach, barbecue, bake, smoke or fry the flesh, or put it in a curry, soup or chowder.

Tarakihi
Nemadactylus macropterus
Tarakihi (see page 124), a popular fish with New Zealanders, can be found all over Aotearoa, most abundantly along the East Cape, around Cook Strait and around the South Island.

They are suitable for most methods of cooking and eating: baked, fried, barbecued or poached, put in a curry, soup or chowder or eaten raw as sashimi.

Warehenga, Kahu, Haku
Yellowtail kingfish
Seriola lalandi
A standard kingfish comes in at 5–15 kilograms, but they can weigh upward of 50 kilograms; in fact, the largest kingfish in the world can be found in Aotearoa's waters. In particular, they are found throughout North Island coastal waters and at the top of the South Island.

They have a distinctive white underside with a green-gold band running along the length of the fish. The dark colouration of the flesh lightens on cooking. Kingfish fillets hold their shape when cooked and are suitable to bake, barbecue, fry, smoke, casserole, poach or steam, or to eat raw and in sushi.

Warehou
Common warehou, blue warehou
Seriolella brama
Blue warehou is a small to medium-sized fish, generally weighing 1–3 kilograms, with a blue-green topside and silver underside, small head and pointed pectoral fins.

They are most abundant around the South Island and are mainly fished around Cook Strait and the West Coast. They grow rapidly and have a lifespan of about 10 years.

Blue warehou feed indiscriminately on salp, krill, crabs and small squid, at depths of 20–200 metres.

ĪNANGA
Whitebait
Galaxias maculatus
LOCATED: ACROSS AOTEAROA

Īnanga (see page 126, top left) is the Māori word for whitebait, the collective term for five species of Galaxiidae: īnanga, kōaro, banded kōkopu, giant kōkopu and shortjaw kōkopu. Īnanga, or īnaka, are small freshwater fish that live in streams and rivers close to the ocean.

Māori traditionally caught īnanga by setting out finely woven nets made from stripped harakeke. The tiny fish were cooked in a hāngi or over an open fire, or preserved by being laid on mats in the sun to dry.

Before Europeans arrived in Aotearoa, īnanga were abundant in most parts of the country, particularly on the West Coast of the South Island. By the mid-1800s, īnanga were being heavily fished by both Māori and Europeans. In some cases supply outweighed demand and the excess catch was repurposed as garden fertiliser or animal feed. Several īnanga canneries were established and operating at the turn of the 20th century, but slowly disappeared with the arrival of refrigeration. In the 1930s, fishermen along the Waikato River paid a voluntary īnanga tax when fishing in the river – for every pound of īnanga caught and sold, they paid one penny toward the expenses of the Kīngitanga, or Māori King Movement.

Today, īnanga are New Zealand's most expensive and even controversial fish. Four of the five species are threatened and some scientists warn that they will be extinct within the next generation unless drastic measures are put in place to strictly regulate harvesting. However, others say there's no evidence of decline. There have never been any limits on recreational or commercial īnanga fishing, meaning the lack of official catch records makes it hard to measure historical īnanga population numbers over time. Some small towns, particularly along the West Coast, rely on the income that comes with the īnanga season – for example, 'baiting' jobs, tourism, the sale of raw and prepared īnanga products, and the manufacture and sale of nets.

The government roll-out of new laws regulating the wild harvesting of īnanga seems inevitable and necessary. In the meantime, sustainably farmed īnanga are becoming available year-round.

KARENGO, PARENGO
Red nori
Pyropia columbina
LOCATED: INTERTIDAL ROCKS ACROSS AOTEAROA

Karengo (see page 126, top right) is a seaweed that can be found growing on intertidal rocks along exposed coastlines. Māori valued it highly for being a great source of protein and it's still harvested for these reasons. Karengo, related to Japanese nori, is harvested in winter months and dried to be used throughout the year. It has a salty, fishy taste when dried but is very mild (like lettuce) when eaten fresh.

Commercial karengo harvesting was permitted along the Kaikōura coast of the South Island until a massive earthquake lifted the seabed in November 2016. This shift, which was up to 2 metres upwards in some places, pushed several kilometres of precious marine life and seaweed to the surface where it could not survive. An indefinite ban on recreational and commercial seaweed harvesting has been put in place to help Kaikōura's marine ecosystem recover.

KEKENO
New Zealand fur seal
Arctocephalus forsteri
LOCATED: SOUTH ISLAND, RAKIURA STEWART ISLAND, NEW ZEALAND SUBANTARCTIC ISLANDS

Humans have not been kind to Aotearoa's kekeno population. Kekeno were a prized catch for early Māori. They provided a bountiful supply of tender, juicy meat that was most often cooked in hāngi. Māori also turned seals' teeth into fish hooks and made kahu kekeno (seal cloaks) from their skins. By the time the first Europeans

arrived during the 1700s, using kekeno skins for cloaks had been cast aside in favour of softer materials like kurī skins or kiwi feathers.

Captain Cook's arrival sparked the start of a kekeno-hunting rush. News spread throughout the British colonies that New Zealand was blessed with an endless supply of fur seals, which were sought-after for their pelts and fat. It wasn't long before sealing parties from Australia, England and the US descended on Aotearoa to hunt as many as they could. This new industry disturbed more than just the seal populations. In southern parts of New Zealand there were a number of violent skirmishes between Māori and European sealers and over 70 people died as a result.

By the end of the 19th century, kekeno were on the verge of extinction, and seal hunting was outlawed in 1893. While the kekeno population has recovered, it's nowhere near pre-colonisation levels. Hunting may be banned but marine pollution and tourism ventures are proving troublesome to the kekeno's favoured habitats. Kekeno are also at risk from commercial trawling operators, who inadvertently catch them in their nets and leave them to drown.

KINA

New Zealand sea urchin
Evechinus chloroticus
LOCATED: ACROSS AOTEAROA

Kina (see page 129) is the Māori name for a type of sea urchin unique to Aotearoa. Māori have been harvesting kina for hundreds of years and consider the creamy yellow-orange roe hidden within its spiky shell to be a great delicacy. Māori usually ate kina raw, but occasionally it would be placed directly onto the embers of a fire and left to cook until the roe was very hot.

Kina are widespread throughout Aotearoa and more than 600 tonnes are harvested by recreational and commercial fishers each year. While New Zealand's wild-caught kina haven't been a hit internationally (they sometimes have a slight sourness or a brown shade to the roe), they can fetch substantial prices on the local market.

KŌURA

Freshwater crayfish
Paranephrops planifrons, Paranephrops zealandicus
LOCATED: ACROSS AOTEAROA

Kōura (see page 130, top left) are one of Aotearoa's most prized delicacies, a national treasure best prepared as simply as possible. There are two endemic species: *Paranephrops planifrons* (northern kōura)

and *Paranephrops zealandicus* (southern kōura).

Kōura are masters of camouflage, often found hiding between rocks and stones of our lakes, streams and ponds. Kōura was almost always present whenever there was a gathering at a pā. As well as being a food source, it was given to visiting kaumātua from other iwi. Kōura were caught by leaving bait (such as kina or pāua) in small net bags called tōrehe. Once the kōura had crawled inside, the gatherer would draw the mouth of the bag shut and take home the bounty.

In recent years, overfishing and pollution have had a negative effect on the kōura population – they are now considered endangered. Despite this, you don't need a recreational fishing permit to gather them (though there is a daily limit on how many a person can take). Kōura are slow-growing creatures that take up to four years to reach 2 centimetres in length. Don't be greedy when gathering them – take a couple and leave the rest for future generations.

KUKU, KŪTAI

Green-lipped or greenshell mussels
Perna canaliculus
LOCATED: ACROSS AOTEAROA

Kuku (see page 130, top right), or kūtai as they are sometimes known, are one of Aotearoa's most iconic and economically important seafoods.

Māori have been harvesting the abundant and readily available kuku for centuries. Thanks to their natural habitat, kuku were harvested by both young and old. The plump flesh was either eaten fresh or dried and stored away for leaner times. The shells were used to prepare harakeke for weaving, or in jewellery.

They can be found in almost all coastal parts of New Zealand, below the intertidal zone. These endemic shellfish are much larger than most mussel species, some growing to more than 20 centimetres long, with sweet, juicy flesh.

Kuku are Aotearoa's second biggest seafood export, worth more than $250 million annually. Recreational harvesting is permitted in most parts of the country – you don't need a permit – but strict regulations regarding minimum legal size and daily bag limits must be observed.

PĀUA
Blackfoot abalone
Haliotis iris
LOCATED: ACROSS AOTEAROA

Pāua is an endemic abalone found all across Aotearoa. It's known for its iridescent shell insides and the thin black surface layer that coats the meat.

Pāua (see page 130, bottom right) has a rich history in Aotearoa and has become something of a culinary delicacy. Māori have been harvesting pāua as a food source for centuries, often keeping the shell to be used in carvings and jewellery.

In Māori mythology, pāua began life without a shell. All the other sea creatures made fun of pāua for being unsightly and slow. Tangaroa, the god of the sea, saw the hardship pāua was enduring and decided to create a beautiful coat for it. He decorated it with shades of blue from the ocean and asked his brother Tāne, god of the forest, for the lushest greens. When the other sea creatures saw pāua's new coat, they were jealous and destroyed it. So Tangaroa made the coat again, strengthening it so it would be impossible for any sea creature to break. He covered it with barnacles and moss to camouflage the ocean-blue and forest-green mosaic of the shell so pāua could live undisturbed.

In the modern world, pāua is a high-demand, high-priced commodity. Pāua numbers were hit hard by overharvesting in the second half of the 20th century, so strict regulations were put in place for both recreational and commercial harvesting. Population numbers have risen as a result, but so too have the prices. But the steep prices are all part of a necessary change in attitude toward the protection – and value – of our kaimoana. Unfortunately, not everyone is as keen on kaimoana protection as we are. The high prices have attracted illegal poachers, who make millions of dollars by selling up to 400 tonnes of pāua on the black market every year.

PIPI
Paphies australis

TUANGI, TUAKI
Cockles
Austrovenus stutchburyi

TUATUA
Paphies subtriangulata
ALL LOCATED: ACROSS AOTEAROA

Tuatua (see page 130, bottom left) and pipi are two of the most popular kaimoana consumed in modern restaurants. Endemic to Aotearoa, they can be found buried in the sand of ocean beaches all around the country. Both were a staple food source for Māori living in coastal areas. Tuatua and pipi are closely related to the legendary toheroa, though they're much smaller in size and have a sweeter flavour.

While pipi and tuatua look very similar, they are two different clams. The way to tell them apart is by looking at the shell and hinge: tuatua have an asymmetrical shell with an off-centre hinge, while pipi shells are symmetrical and have a centred hinge.

Recreational harvesting is permitted in most areas of Aotearoa but the legal bag limit is different depending on local council regulations. The best time to collect tuatua and pipi is at low tide, by digging your toes into the sand and feeling for patches of shells. Once you've found some, dig down with your hands and pull them out. Keep them alive in a bucket of seawater for 24 hours before eating them – they will spit out any excess sand.

Tuangi, also known as tuaki, are commonly found on beaches near estuaries where mud levels in the sand are higher. Despite commonly being called cockles, they're actually littleneck clams from the venus clam family. Tuangi are widespread in Aotearoa and population numbers are stable – daily bag limits are as much as 150 per person per day in some areas. Tuangi are also commercially harvested and can be found in most supermarkets and restaurants around the country.

PŪPŪ
Sea snails
Amphibola crenata
LOCATED: ACROSS AOTEAROA

Pūpū (see page 126, bottom right) is an umbrella term for three different kinds of edible snails that live on the Australasian seabed. Their protective shells often have beautiful patterns and interesting etchings all over them.

There are three distinct categories of pūpū: herbivores, which mainly survive on seaweed and are found around rocky coastlines; coastal carnivores like whelks, rock shells and oyster borers, which hunt in subtidal zones; and other carnivorous snails that float around the sea and prey on jellyfish.

These sea creatures were an important food source for Māori and appear in many legends. They were lifesavers in a tale involving Whaitiri, an evil old woman from the South Island who was notorious for feasting on her own family members. One night, two of her grandsons stayed over. Afraid of being eaten alive, they found some kanohi pūpū (cat's eye snails) and slept with them over their eyes. The old woman thought the two boys were awake all night and left them alone.

RIMURAPA
Bull kelp
Durvillaea antarctica
LOCATED: COASTAL SOUTH ISLAND

Rimurapa (see page 126, bottom left) was primarily used as a means of storing, cooking and transporting food. The thicker blades would be sliced open, inflated and dried to create a bag (pōhā). These pōhā were often packed with some form of high-fat protein, such as native birds, seal or kiore, which were then covered in their own rendered fat. The pōhā were sealed and stored for later use. If done correctly, food preserved this way was said to have a shelf life of three to six years. Rimurapa was also used to wrap food before it went into a hāngi.

Rimurapa could also be eaten – the blade of the plant was roasted and chewed, or the dried kelp was mixed with the juice of tutu berries to make a highly coveted jelly.

TIO PARUPARU
Bluff oysters
Ostrea chilensis
LOCATED: FOVEAUX STRAIT, SOUTHLAND

For oyster fanatics, the start of the tio paruparu season in March is treated with great excited. The huge oysters are the only ones in the world still dredged in the wild and their short six-month season makes them even more precious. Their razor-sharp, barnacle-encrusted shells are notoriously difficult to shuck open – ask most New Zealand chefs about tio paruparu and it's almost always the first thing they'll bring up.

Tio paruparu (see page 135) are now internationally renowned for their meatiness and brininess, but southern Māori have been eating them for hundreds of years. They are a taonga species to the Ngāi Tahu iwi, for whom the oyster has a deep spiritual and cultural importance.

Commercial harvesting began in the 1860s along Foveaux Strait, a wide channel of stormy, wind-blown water that separates Rakiura Stewart Island from mainland Aotearoa. Dredging also began soon after, along the coast of Rakiura at

Port William and Halfmoon Bay.

Commercial activities were halted after only a few years due to overharvesting, with seabeds that were once rich in tio paruparu found almost empty. In 1879, with oyster numbers seemingly on the mend, commercial dredging resumed and moved away from Rakiura toward the small town of Bluff. It's here that they earned the nickname Bluff oyster. Despite the earlier lessons of overharvesting, it was another 84 years before a quota system was put in place.

Tio paruparu continue to be harvested commercially for local and international markets. Numbers remain strong, despite threats from pollution and parasites such as *Bonamia ostreae*, a lethal infection that can wipe out entire shellfish colonies in a matter of months. The famous southern delicacy has proven to be as resilient as the shell in which it resides.

TOHEROA
Paphies ventricosa
LOCATED: ACROSS AOTEAROA

Toheroa (see page 136) is a large endemic surf clam that was once abundant in New Zealand – our tinned toheroa soup was world-famous – but it has been overharvested to the point of near extinction.

The word toheroa literally means 'long tongue'. Māori had eaten toheroa

for centuries but its population numbers took a rapid dive post-colonisation, as European settlers quickly caught on to its deliciousness. In the 1920s, recreational toheroa harvesting (with a limit of 50 toheroa per person per day) was permitted 10 months of the year. Commercial harvesting allowances were even higher. Northland factories canned 20–70 tonnes per year, which were sold in New Zealand and internationally. There was an insatiable demand for toheroa, which was further intensified when Prince Edward VIII broke royal protocol during his 1921 visit by asking for a second serving of toheroa soup. This small act made newspapers around the world and the toheroa industry boomed.

By the 1950s, toheroa numbers had significantly decreased. Stricter recreational quotas reduced the season to just two months of the year, with a new daily allowance of 20 per person per day. This came too late; by the mid-1960s, the toheroa population was at crisis point. Commercial harvesting was banned in 1969. Recreational harvesting was allowed to continue for another decade but was ultimately made illegal in 1979.

Customary rights granted to Māori remain the only exception to this ban. Toheroa can be harvested for special occasions such as a hui (meeting) or tangi, but even this requires a permit and the numbers that can be gathered are very limited.

The toheroa population has not recovered to anything like the previous levels, despite the bans. And overharvesting hasn't been the only culprit. The weight of vehicles driving along the beach crushes juvenile shellfish and unsettles adult toheroa living beneath the surface of the sand. Environmental changes have also had adverse effects. Toheroa need fresh water to regulate their temperature and moisture levels. In some areas, fresh water running down to beaches from inland streams has become polluted or dried up. Illegal poaching has also been an ongoing issue, despite hefty fines imposed on those caught.

It is unlikely that we'll see toheroa back on the menu in our lifetime. This should serve as a warning to all of us of what happens when we're reckless with our natural resources.

TUNA
Freshwater eel
***Anguilla dieffenbachii* (longfin eel),
Anguilla australis (shortfin eel)**
LOCATED: ACROSS AOTEAROA

Tuna (see page 138) have been living in Aotearoa's rivers and streams for over 23 million years and have great importance in Māori culture. They are seen as a link to the gods; marae carvings of tuna often appear beside carvings of ancestors to signal the importance of the person

portrayed. There are numerous Māori stories, waiata (songs) and whakataukī (proverbs) referencing tuna as a central character. Māori had more than 100 names to describe their different colours and sizes. Te hopu tuna (eeling) could be done by hand or by using weirs, pots and spears. More information about these methods can be found on pages 42–43.

Tuna were a key food source. Tuna was preserved using a technique called 'ahi rara tuna' – this involved cleaning and bleeding several tuna, removing the heads and backbones, then laying them on a grate over a fire so they would cook and dry. Once this process was complete, the tuna would be stored away for future use. Quicker preparation methods – such as simply cooking them over a fire – were used if the tuna were to be eaten immediately.

Pollution, historical overfishing and loss of habitat have all contributed to a drop in Aotearoa's tuna population. Māori have customary rights to fish tuna in their rohe (region) for special occasions, such as hui or tangi. However, many choose not to as they prefer to leave the tuna to reproduce and grow in numbers.

Commercial eeling was once a bustling industry in Aotearoa but has been on a steady decline in more recent years. Tuna were commercially overfished in the past but, since being placed under the Quota Management System, commercial eeleries must now adhere to strict regulations regarding catch sizes, limits and reporting. More often than not, these eeleries use less than half of their quota allowance. The biggest threat to tuna is not commercial fishing but the pollution pumped into our waterways from human activity.

WHAKAHAO
New Zealand sea lion, Hooker's sea lion
Phocarctos hookeri
LOCATED: AUCKLAND AND CAMPBELL ISLANDS

Whakahao were an important food source for Māori and they were hunted heavily before European sealers arrived. The explosion of the local sealing industry in the 1800s saw whakahao (along with kekeno) hunted to near extinction. Whakahao hunting, and seal hunting more broadly, was banned in 1893.

Today, there are fewer than 12,000 whakahao in existence: they are considered the world's rarest sea lion species. Population numbers are critically low and it's extremely rare to see whakahao along the coasts of mainland New Zealand. Their preferred habitat is Aotearoa's subantarctic Auckland and Campbell islands.

WHEKE
New Zealand octopus
LOCATED: ACROSS AOTEAROA

Aotearoa's waters boast 42 wheke species, nearly two-thirds of which are endemic. Wheke (see page 141) often represent whānau or iwi in Māori symbolism, and also feature in a number of myths and legends. In the most famous, that of Kupe and Te Wheke-o-Muturangi, the famous explorer Kupe fought a giant wheke all the way across the Pacific Ocean, which led him to his discovery of Aotearoa.

Traditionally, Māori caught wheke by hand. This was done by placing one hand in the water and allowing the wheke to wrap its tentacles around it, then pulling the creature from the water and killing it.

3 —

THE
RECIPES

He kai kei aku ringa

*There is food
at the end of my hands*

SAVOURY

RĒWENA FLATBREAD
WITH TĪTĪ FAT BUTTER

SERVES 8

Flour was not available to pre-European Māori, but the bread that emerged after its arrival is unique to our culture. Rēwena is a sourdough using taewa or kūmara as the 'bug' (starter). It's usually baked into loaves, but I've always had a love affair with flatbread that comes straight off a hot grill – the smell, the char, the chewiness.

FOR THE REWENA STARTER:
200 g urenika potatoes, scrubbed and diced
200 g high-grade flour
20 g sugar
2 g fresh yeast

Put the potatoes in a pot, set over medium heat and cover with cold water. Bring to a boil then cover with a lid and leave to cook until soft (about 10–15 minutes). Remove from the heat, mash the potatoes and allow to cool to room temperature.

Mix in the sugar, flour and yeast, then transfer to a large container. Cover with a perforated lid to allow the starter to breathe. You'll need to feed the starter every 1–2 days (see the rēwena starter food below). The longer a starter is left to ferment the better. I'll generally wait at least a week before making my first loaf from a fresh starter.

FOR THE REWENA STARTER FOOD:
100 ml tepid water
5 g sugar
100 g high-grade flour

Mix these ingredients into the rēwena starter every 1–2 days. Keep the starter in a cool, dry place.

NOTE: For every fifth feed, cook and mash two urenika potatoes and add them to your starter food. Use the water you've cooked the potatoes instead of regular water.

FOR THE REWENA FLATBREAD:
6 g fresh yeast
190 ml tepid water
150 g rēwena starter
5 g mānuka honey
300 g plain flour, plus more for dusting
3 g fennel seeds, toasted
3 g cumin seeds, toasted
50 g kūmara, peeled, roasted and diced
10 g salt
100 g tītī fat

Whisk together the yeast and water. When the yeast has dissolved, stir in the rēwena starter and honey. In a separate bowl, whisk together the flour, fennel, cumin and kūmara. Combine with the yeast mixture and mix well, to form a dough. Cover loosely with a plate or damp cloth and leave to ferment for 30 minutes, then stir through the salt until it dissolves. Let the dough rise for 30 minutes, then gently fold the dough over itself, first from the north, then south, east and west. Cover loosely and let rest for 30 minutes. Repeat this folding and resting process twice more, then cover the dough and leave to ferment overnight in the fridge.

The next day, let the dough sit at room temperature for about 30 minutes. Dust a tray with white flour and divide the dough into small balls of about 50 g each. Gently flatten the balls by hand and brush each side with tītī fat. Cook gently on a grill or in a pan drizzled with oil, for about five minutes each side. Brush the bread with tītī fat as it cooks. Serve warm with tītī fat butter (see page 148).

FOR THE TITI FAT BUTTER:
200 g unsalted butter, at room temperature
100 g tītī fat
Salt, to taste

Using a stand mixer fitted with a whisk, beat the
unsalted butter until pale and fluffy; stop the mixer
every now and then to scrape down the sides.
With the machine running, slowly drizzle in the
tītī fat so it emulsifies together with the butter.
If you can't get tītī fat, duck fat or lamb fat works
just as well. Once all the fat is in, leave it to mix for
another minute. Season with salt to taste and serve
immediately.

 If not using straight away, store in an airtight
container in the fridge. Bring to room temperature
when needed then beat using the stand mixer and
whisk attachment for one minute.

CRUMBED AVOCADO, KARAMŪ VINAIGRETTE

SERVES 4

This dish featured on the Hiakai menu as an ode to Mount Pihanga, the maiden mountain in the 'Battle of the Mountains', the story of seven male mountains vying for her love. We wanted this dish to be luscious and feminine, much like Pihanga herself, and we incorporated plants commonly found on the mountain.

FOR THE CRUMBED AVOCADO:
1 T vegetable oil
50 g sunflower seeds
50 g pumpkin seeds
10 g mamaku ash (see below)
1 avocado, peeled and pitted
Pine Oil (see page 256)
Flaky sea salt
Black pepper, freshly ground

Heat the oil in a small pan and toast the seeds until golden. Remove from the heat and allow to cool, then season with salt. Roughly chop and mix with mamaku ash and salt.

Brush the avocado with a little Pine Oil, then coat with the seed mixture. Cut into 2 cm slices when ready to serve.

TO MAKE MAMAKU ASH:
Grill the peeled skin from a mamaku tree fern in a wood oven to give it a smoky flavour, then dry overnight in a dehydrator set to 70°C. The next day, grind it to a powder in a blender. Store in an airtight container until ready to use.

FOR THE CHARRED ZUCCHINI AND SNOW PEA PURÉE:
Baking soda
100 g snow peas, plus 50 g for garnishing
80 ml Pine Oil (see page 256)
1 lemon, freshly squeezed
Flaky sea salt
100 g zucchini
Canola oil
250 ml vegetable stock

Bring a small pot of water to the boil. Add a pinch of baking soda then blanch 100 g of snow peas for 40–60 seconds. Drain and transfer to a bowl of ice-cold water. Transfer the peas to a blender and add the Pine Oil. Purée until smooth, then season to taste with lemon juice and salt. Strain through a fine sieve and store in a squeezy bottle.

Brush the zucchini with a little canola oil and season with salt. Char in a wood oven or on a grill. When it's cooked, remove from the oven or grill and cool. When it's cool enough, slice into very fine ribbons, ideally with a mandoline.

Cut the remaining snow peas into fine julienne slices. Blanch in boiling vegetable stock for 5 seconds then transfer to ice-cold water. Drain and set aside until ready to use.

FOR THE KARAMŪ VINAIGRETTE:

1 bunch fresh karamū leaves

2 g chilli flakes

4 g coriander seeds

2 shallots, diced

3 g miro leaves

10 g fresh ginger

3 T mānuka honey

2 lemons, freshly squeezed

50 ml Karamū Vinegar (see page 252)

2 T cornflour, mixed with 1 T water

Put the karamū leaves in a large pot with 2 litres of water. Bring to a boil, then remove from the heat and leave to infuse until cool. Strain into a new pot and add all the remaining ingredients except the cornflour. Set over medium heat and boil for 10 minutes, then remove from the heat. Strain into a clean vessel (discard the solids) and whisk in the cornflour. Season to taste with salt.

TO ASSEMBLE:

Micro herbs and flowers

Put two slices of avocado on each plate and season with salt. Add three ribbons of zucchini, then pea purée, sliced peas, and micro herbs (for example: sorrel, purple shiso, marigolds). Drizzle with karamū vinaigrette and serve.

ROASTED CAULIFLOWER, MANONO SAUCE, LŪʻAU

SERVES 4

At Hiakai, our nickname for manono is 'Aotearoa Turmeric', so it seems only natural that we'd eventually make a curry-like sauce involving the ingredient. This dish was on the menu at Hiakai during our first winter in operation – it's warming and comforting, perfect for cold nights.

FOR THE MANONO SAUCE:

1 T vegetable oil
1 white onion, peeled and diced
15 g fresh ginger, peeled and finely diced
¼ cauliflower, diced
2 T manono bark powder (see page 263)
1 T piri piri chilli
1 T mānuka honey
Table salt, to taste
500 ml coconut cream
25 ml freshly squeezed lime juice

Set a large, shallow pan over medium heat. Add the oil, followed by the onion, ginger and cauliflower. Sauté until golden, then stir through the manono, piri piri and honey. Season to taste with the salt, then pour in the coconut cream. Bring to a gentle boil and top with a baking-paper cartouche (or a lid left slightly ajar). Lower the heat and cook gently until the cauliflower is very soft. Transfer to a high-speed blender and purée until smooth. Taste and adjust the seasoning with the lime juice, plus more salt, honey or piri piri.

FOR THE PICKLED CAULIFLOWER:

1 L white wine vinegar
500 g white sugar
100 g table salt
¼ large cauliflower, broken into florets and shaved into 2 mm slices with a mandoline

Put the vinegar, sugar and salt in a saucepan set over medium heat. Bring to the boil, stirring to dissolve the sugar and salt, then remove from the heat and leave to cool. Pour into a bowl or jar and add the shaved cauliflower. Cover and store in the fridge for 24 hours before using.

FOR THE LŪʻAU:

4 large taro leaves, washed well, stems discarded
1 T vegetable oil
2 cloves garlic, peeled and sliced
500 ml coconut cream

Roll up the taro leaves and slice them into 5 mm strips. Set a medium-sized pot over medium heat and add the oil, followed by the garlic. Cook until golden, then add the taro leaves. Sauté until they collapse and turn dark green/brown. Pour in the coconut cream and season with salt. Cover and cook on a very low heat for at least 1 hour, stirring every 10–15 minutes to prevent the leaves burning on the bottom of the pot. The lūʻau is ready when the leaves are completely soft and combined with the coconut cream.

FOR THE SUNFLOWER SEED CRACKER:
125 g sunflower seeds
60 g egg whites
20 g caster sugar
Sea salt

Heat the oven to 170°C. Spread the sunflower seeds on a tray and bake for 10 minutes, then set aside to cool.

Whisk the egg whites until stiff, then gradually whisk in the sugar to form a stiff meringue. Fold in the sunflower seeds. Let the mixture drain through a tamis or drum sieve until just enough egg white remains to hold the seeds together. Spread this mixture thinly over a tray lined with a silicone mat or well-greased baking paper. Sprinkle with sea salt and bake for 15 minutes. Remove from the oven and carefully flip over using a long metal spatula. Bake for another 15 minutes, until lightly golden. Cool and store in an airtight container.

FOR THE ROASTED CAULIFLOWER:
1 cauliflower, cut into four

Wrap each piece of cauliflower in foil. Roast over a barbecue for about 30 minutes, or until slightly soft. Remove from the heat and unwrap.

Deep-fry the cauliflower pieces at 180°C until golden. Trim off any burnt parts before serving.

TO ASSEMBLE:
Micro sorrel

Cut each cauliflower portion in half, then press the halves together with a tablespoon of lū'au. Roast in a 180°C oven for 5 minutes. Then arrange the cauliflower on four small plates. Sprinkle each serving with four pickled cauliflower shavings and 4–5 pieces of sunflower cracker. Spoon with manono sauce, garnish with micro sorrel and serve immediately.

FRIED HUHU GRUBS, KŪMARA GNOCCHI, HUHU SAUCE

SERVES 4

Huhu grubs have a mild nuttiness that made me think of satay sauce when I first tried them. I created a sauce with roasted huhus, and to my surprise it tasted a lot like a chestnut sauce we served with agnolotti at A Voce, in New York. I decided to serve the sauce with a kūmara gnocchi as a tribute to my time working the pasta section at A Voce.

FOR THE KŪMARA GNOCCHI:

200 g kūmara, roasted and mashed
30 g Parmesan, finely grated
125 g buckwheat flour, plus extra for rolling
¾ T salt
Finely grated zest of 1 lemon
2 T olive oil
Salt, to taste
2 T vegetable oil
Black pepper, freshly ground

Using your hands, mix together the mashed kūmara, Parmesan, buckwheat flour, salt and lemon zest. Knead mixture with your hands until a sticky dough forms. Divide in half.

Dust a work surface with buckwheat flour. Roll each portion of dough into a long rope, then cut into 2 cm pieces.

Bring a large pot of water to the boil. Add the olive oil and a generous spoonful of salt. Cook the gnocchi in batches for about 3 minutes. Remove with a slotted spoon, then drop them into a bowl of iced water. Drain gnocchi and arrange on a lined tray. Leave uncovered in the fridge overnight.

When you're ready to serve, set a sauté pan over medium-hot heat and add the vegetable oil. When it's hot, add 1–2 handfuls of gnocchi and sauté until golden brown and hot in the middle. Season with salt and black pepper and serve immediately.

FOR THE HUHU SAUCE:

1 T vegetable oil
15 huhu grubs
1 small white onion, peeled and finely diced
2 cloves garlic, peeled and finely diced
50 g peanuts, roasted and shelled
½ tsp dried horopito flakes (see page 262)
100 ml chicken stock
250 ml cream
Flaky sea salt
Ground white pepper
Freshly squeezed lime juice

Set a saucepan over medium heat. Add the oil, followed by the huhu grubs. Toast the grubs for 1 minute, then stir in the onion, garlic and peanuts. Sauté until the onions are soft and caramelised. Stir in the horopito flakes, chicken stock and cream. Simmer gently for 15 minutes. Remove from the heat and pour into a high-speed blender and purée until smooth. Season with flaky sea salt, ground white pepper and a few drops of lime juice. Pour the sauce through a fine mesh sieve and serve hot.

FOR THE FRIED HUHU GRUBS:

25 g unsalted butter
2 T vegetable oil
1 clove garlic, peeled and finely diced
12 huhu grubs
Flaky sea salt

Set a cast-iron pan over medium heat and add the butter and oil. When the butter starts to bubble and brown, stir in the garlic and huhu grubs. Cook for about 30 seconds, until crispy. Remove from the heat and transfer the huhu to a paper towel-lined tray. Season with flaky sea salt and serve immediately.

TO ASSEMBLE:

Smoked pecorino
Micro cress
Toasted breadcrumbs
Olive oil

Place 3–4 spoonfuls of huhu sauce in each bowl. Divide the kūmara gnocchi between the bowls, then top with three huhu grubs. Sprinkle with a little freshly grated smoked pecorino and garnish with micro cress, toasted breadcrumbs and a few drops of olive oil.

KAMOKAMO, TAHINI YOGHURT, PUFFED WILD RICE

SERVES 2

This dish is all about simplicity. Kamokamo is an underrated vegetable that often gets put into soups and broths as an afterthought. I wanted to make a dish that placed kamkamo as the hero, as opposed to a gourd hidden amongst a mélange of other flavours.

FOR THE SOY GLAZE:

70 ml soy sauce
130 ml mirin
20 g miso
50 g sugar
10 ml lemon juice

Put the soy, mirin, miso and sugar in a small pot set over medium heat. Simmer until it reaches the consistency of a light syrup. Stir in the lemon juice and remove from the heat.

FOR THE TAHINI YOGHURT:

50 g pumpkin seeds
12 ml sunflower oil
80 g thick, natural Greek yoghurt
Salt, to taste

Heat the oven to 180°C. Spread the pumpkin seeds on a tray and bake for 10–15 minutes, until golden. Tip into a blender and add the sunflower oil. Blend until smooth then scrape into a bowl. Season to taste. Mix about a tablespoon of this mixture through the Greek yoghurt and adjust the seasoning with salt. Store in the fridge until required.

FOR THE PUFFED WILD RICE:

75 ml sunflower oil
2 tsp black wild rice
Salt

Pour the sunflower oil into a small pot and heat to 190°C. Set up a small metal bowl with a metal sieve resting on top (use a trivet if necessary to keep the sieve from touching the bottom of the bowl).

Test the temperature of the oil using a thermometer. When ready, drop the rice into the oil (it should puff up instantly), then transfer to the sieve. Season with salt and allow to cool. When cold, transfer to an airtight container lined with paper towels. Store at room temperature.

FOR THE KAMOKAMO:

1 kamokamo, washed and cut in half

Wrap the kamokamo halves in foil and set on a grill (on a grill pan) for 15 minutes each side, or until they soften. Carefully unwrap and allow to cool on a rack, then cut into 200 g cross-section portions.

Brush the kamokamo with soy glaze and sear on each side until lightly charred. Remove from the heat and brush again with the soy glaze, then place on a tray.

TO ASSEMBLE:

Spoon a generous tablespoon of tahini yoghurt on top of each piece of kamokamo. Top with about 2 tablespoons of puffed rice. Transfer to a plate and spoon over 1 teaspoon of soy glaze. Garnish with micro sorrel and serve.

RAW BLUFF OYSTERS, WAKAME, OYSTER EMULSION

MAKES 6

This preparation came about after one of my chefs shucked a couple dozen Bluffs but had a number of mishaps along the way, which meant some of them weren't pretty enough to serve. Not wanting to discard the damaged ones, I turned them into a dressing, which delivers an even greater punch of Bluff brininess to the oysters.

FOR THE BLUFF OYSTER EMULSION:
3 freshly shucked oysters, with the juice (discard any shell)
1 small shallot, peeled and diced
30 ml white wine vinegar
150 ml neutral vegetable oil
5 ml freshly squeezed lemon juice
Flaky sea salt, to taste

Put the oysters, oyster juice, shallot and white wine vinegar in a high-speed blender and blend on high for 10 seconds. Keep blending and slowly drizzle in the oil. Once the mixture is smooth and thick enough to coat the back of a spoon, season it with flaky sea salt and lemon juice. Transfer into an airtight container and store in the fridge.

FOR THE PICKLED WAKAME:
250 g sugar
5 black peppercorns
50 ml water
100 ml white wine vinegar
50 g wakame (sea greens), cut into 5 mm squares

Put the sugar, peppercorns, water and white wine vinegar in a saucepan set over medium heat. Bring to the boil, stirring to dissolve the sugar, then remove from the heat and leave to cool. Strain the liquid over the wakame, then cover and store in the fridge until required.

FOR THE KAWAKAWA OIL:
100 ml grapeseed oil
40 g fresh kawakawa leaves, blanched

Put the oil and kawakawa leaves in a high-speed blender and blend until the oil turns emerald green. The oil will get really hot during the blending process. Remove the oil from the machine and place into a bowl and set it over an ice bath. You do this to quickly cool the oil so it doesn't overcook and turn brown. When the oil is cool, pour it through a fine sieve lined with a coffee filter. Pour into a squeezy bottle and store in the fridge until required.

TO ASSEMBLE:
6 oysters
Fresh kōkihi (New Zealand spinach) leaves
Fresh sea celery leaves

Arrange 6 freshly shucked oysters on a bed of salt or ice. Spoon 1 T of oyster emulsion over each oyster, then arrange 3–4 pieces of pickled wakame, kōkihi and sea celery on top. Finish with a few drops of kawakawa oil.

GRILLED BLUFF OYSTERS, PIRI PIRI, LARDONS

MAKES 12

When grilling oysters, you need to pick a species that is robust enough to stand up to the heat. The firmness of Bluff oysters makes them perfect for popping onto a barbecue with a spoonful of dressing or compound butter. This recipe comes from the early pop-up days of Hiakai.

50 g thick-cut pancetta, cut into matchsticks
1 large shallot, peeled and finely diced
1 clove garlic, peeled and finely diced
1 T piri piri paste
Freshly squeezed juice and zest of 1 lime
Flaky sea salt
12 Bluff oysters, shucked and kept in the half shell

Set a small sauté pan over medium heat. Add the pancetta and allow to cook until the fat renders out, stirring to ensure it caramelises evenly. Add the shallots, garlic and piri piri paste to the pan. Cook until the shallots have softened and started to turn golden brown. Add the lime juice and zest, then remove from the heat. Season with a little flaky sea salt and keep warm until needed.

When you're ready to serve, bring a charcoal grill or barbecue up to a high heat. Put the oysters on the grill in their shells and cook for 1 minute, until the residual oyster juices in the shell start to bubble. Spoon 1 teaspoon of the piri piri dressing onto each oyster and cook for another 30 seconds. When the dressing starts to bubble, remove from the heat and serve immediately.

MOEMOE VICHYSSOISE, KUKU ICE CREAM

SERVES 4

Moemoe can be hard to come by, so we bought half a ton without having a dish in mind. Then, as I was painting the stairwell of Hiakai a few weeks from opening, I remembered Anthony Bourdain's passage in *Kitchen Confidential* about trying Vichyssoise as a child. My next thought was, 'what if we made a mussel ice cream to go with it?'.

FOR THE GREEN-LIPPED MUSSEL (KUKU) ICE CREAM:

60 ml mussel stock (from steamed mussels)
500 ml rice milk
4 egg yolks
10 g trimoline
10 g glucose
3 T dried Mussel Powder (see page 263)
2 g xanthan gum
Sea salt, to taste

Combine the mussel stock and rice milk in a saucepan set over medium heat. Bring to a simmer, stirring occasionally, then remove from the heat.

Mix the egg yolks, trimoline and glucose together in a large bowl. If you can't get trimoline you could use glucose syrup or corn syrup, but both are sweeter and may affect the flavour of the dish. Whisk in the warm rice milk, then pour the mixture back into the pot. Cook, stirring constantly, until it thickens (don't let it boil).

Remove from the heat and pour into a clean bowl through a fine sieve. Stir in the Mussel Powder and add sea salt to taste. Use a stick blender to mix in the xanthan gum. Pour through a fine sieve again and allow to cool completely. Transfer to a covered container and chill overnight. The next day, churn in an ice-cream maker until set. It can be used immediately or stored in the freezer until required.

FOR THE MOEMOE VICHYSSOISE:

500 g moemoe potatoes, washed
20 ml sunflower oil
1 leek, white part only, halved and cut into 2 mm slices
1.5 L white vegetable stock
500 ml rice milk
Reserved cooking juices from 1 kg green-lipped mussels (save the cooked mussels for another use)
Salt, white pepper

Peel and dice the moemoe potatoes, then put them in a bowl of water to prevent them browning. Set aside.

Set a large pan over medium heat and add the sunflower oil, followed by the leeks. Cook until the leeks are soft and translucent. Add the drained moemoe, 1 litre vegetable stock and mussel juices. Season with salt and white pepper and cook until the moemoe are about two-thirds cooked. Pour in the rice milk and continue to cook until the potatoes are completely soft.

Use a stick blender to purée the soup until smooth. Taste and adjust the seasoning, then pass through a fine sieve. Allow to cool completely. Use the remaining vegetable stock to adjust the consistency if needed.

FOR THE MOEMOE GARNISH:
500 g moemoe potatoes, washed
50 g rice flour

Heat an oven to 180°C. Roast 300 g whole moemoe potatoes for about 30 minutes, or until cooked. Leave to cool completely, then peel and cut into 4 mm dice.

Peel the remaining moemoe potatoes and cut into 1 mm batons. Roll in the rice flour until well coated. Deep-fry at 180°C until golden and crunchy. Season with salt.

TO ASSEMBLE:
Add 1 teaspoon diced baked moemoe to each of four small soup bowls. Cover with a teaspoon of moemoe crisps (this should be flat and stable). Place a quenelle of mussel ice cream on top and dust lightly with dried mussel powder. At the table, pour about 150 ml of vichyssoise into each bowl.

KINA PANNA COTTA, SMOKED WAREHOU, KUKU

SERVES 10

The salty-briny-creaminess of kina is one of my favourite flavour profiles. In Aotearoa, kina is a pricey commodity commonly sold in pottles. These are usually 2 parts kina loaf, 1 part kina juice, and people often discard the juice after draining. This recipe came about as a way to use a pottle of kina for maximum flavour and minimal waste.

FOR THE PANNA COTTA:

950 ml cream
500 ml milk
4 star anise
30 g gelatin leaves
400 g kina
40 ml fish sauce
40 ml soy sauce
Salt

Set a medium-sized pot over medium heat. Pour in the cream and milk and add the star anise. Bring to a boil, then remove from the heat. Add a pinch of salt and set aside.

Bloom the gelatin leaves separately in cold water. Once soft, wring out excess water and add the leaves to the cream mixture. Let the gelatin dissolve for about 1 minute, then strain mixture through a fine mesh sieve and pour into a blender.

Add the kina and blend until smooth. Check the seasoning and add soy or fish sauce if necessary.

Let the mixture sit at room temperature for 30 minutes (to allow air bubbles to settle).

FOR THE HOT-SMOKED WAREHOU:

50 g brown sugar
50 g coarse sea salt
5 g freshly ground black peppercorns
1 kg warehou fillets, deboned, skin on

Combine the salt, sugar and pepper. Sprinkle this mixture over the fish and allow to cure for 1 hour. Brush half the cure mixture away and smoke the fish in a hot smoker for 15 minutes. Set aside to cool.

FOR THE STEAMED KUKU:

5 garlic cloves, smashed
1 onion, peeled and diced
150 ml dry white wine
150 ml fish stock
30 green-lipped mussels

Put the garlic, onion, stock and wine in a pot and bring to a simmer. Add the mussels, cover tightly and steam for 5 minutes, until the mussels have opened. Discard any that don't open.

FOR THE KAWAKAWA OIL:

300 ml grapeseed oil
80 g kawakawa leaves, blanched in boiling water and refreshed in iced water, then dried

Put the oil and blanched kawakawa leaves in a high-speed blender and blend until emerald green. Chill immediately over an ice bath. When the oil is cool, pass through a fine sieve lined with a coffee filter. Put into a squeezy bottle and store in the fridge.

TO ASSEMBLE:

40–50 pieces samphire, blanched
20–30 small bundles ice plant, blanched
5 tsp caviar or salmon roe
Freshly squeezed lemon juice
Kawakawa oil

Divide the warehou and kuku between 10 small bowls. Pour over the kina mixture and leave to set in the fridge overnight. Garnish with the samphire, ice plant and caviar, then sprinkle over a little lemon juice and a few drops of kawakawa oil.

CONFIT MOKI, KUKU SAUCE, CRISPY SQUID INK

SERVES 4

In the stories of Kupe's travels around Aotearoa, Kupe is exploring Porirua Harbour when he sees a large white stone in the water, which he retrieves to use as an anchor. This dish captures this moment of discovery. A pearlescent piece of moki is our 'stone', served with kuku sauce and crispy squid ink pasta shaped to mimic black seaweed.

FOR THE CELERIAC PURÉE:
2 celeriac, peeled
1 T sunflower oil
1 white onion, peeled and diced
Salt

Juice one celeriac, putting it through a juicer, retaining the pulp and juice. Cut the other one into 5 mm dice. Set a pot over medium heat and add the sunflower oil. Add the onion and cook until translucent, then add the diced celeriac. Cook until the celeriac has softened, then add the celeriac pulp. Cover and reduce the heat to low. Stir every 2–3 minutes, until the celeriac pulp is cooked. Remove from the heat and transfer to a blender. Add the celeriac juice and blend until smooth and silky. Season with salt and pass through a fine sieve. Keep warm until ready to serve.

FOR THE FISHBONE BROTH:
1 T vegetable oil
1 onion, peeled and finely sliced
2 shallots, peeled and finely sliced
2 cloves garlic, peeled and finely diced
2 fennel bulbs, trimmed and shaved (reserve the fronds for garnishing the dish)
50 ml dry white wine
500 ml fish stock
500 g roasted fish bones
1.5 g xanthan powder
50 ml olive oil

Set a large pot over medium heat. Add the vegetable oil, followed by the onion, shallots, garlic and fennel. Sauté until the vegetables start to colour, then pour in the wine. Add the fish stock and bones and simmer until the vegetables are cooked and the stock has reduced by half. Taste and adjust the seasoning. Strain the vegetables and fish bones from the broth.

Discard the vegetables and fish bones then place the broth into a blender and add the xanthan powder. Blend on low-medium speed to emulsify the sauce. Keep the machine at low speed and slowly pour in the olive oil. The mixture should be thick and creamy. Taste and adjust the seasoning if necessary and pass through a fine sieve.

FOR THE KUKU SAUCE:

1 tsp baking soda
1 bunch spinach, washed
250 ml fishbone broth
50 ml kuku stock (from steamed kuku)
Freshly squeezed lemon juice
Salt

Set a medium pot of water over the heat and add the baking soda. Drop in the spinach and cook until very soft. Drain the spinach and plunge into a bowl of iced water. When completely cooled, drain in a fine sieve, pressing with a cheesecloth to remove excess water.

Transfer the blanched spinach to a blender with the fishbone broth and kuku stock. Blend until it's bright green and has a creamy texture. Season with lemon juice and flaky sea salt, then pass through a fine sieve.

FOR THE SQUID INK PASTA:

6 g squid ink
2 g salt
30 ml water
60 g plain flour

Stir together the squid ink, salt and water. Put the flour on a work top and create a well in the middle. Pour in the liquid and knead together until smooth. Using a pasta machine, roll the dough to 2 mm thick. Hand-cut into ribbons (approx. 5 mm wide × 150 mm long).

Deep-fry 5–10 ribbons at a time in a deep-fryer heated to 180°C. Agitate with a metal spoon to ensure they don't stick together. Once cooked and crunchy, transfer the pasta to a paper-towel-lined tray.

FOR THE PICKLED ICE PLANT:

25 g caster sugar
2 g table salt
50 ml white wine vinegar
30 g ice plant, divided into two stems

Put the sugar, salt and vinegar in a small pot set over medium heat. Bring to a simmer, stirring until the sugar and salt are dissolved. Add the ice plant, then remove from the heat and allow to cool completely before using.

FOR THE YUZU CAVIAR:

300 ml vegetable oil
60 ml yuzu juice
6 g sugar
2 g agar

Pour the vegetable oil into a deep container and leave in the fridge overnight (or for 3 hours in the freezer).

Put the yuzu juice and sugar in a small pot set over low heat. Add the agar and bring to the boil, whisking constantly. Boil for 3 minutes, then remove from the heat and leave to cool until almost set.

Using a tablespoon, pour the mixture drop by drop into the chilled vegetable oil. Let the pearls set in the oil for 2–3 minutes, then lift them out and rinse them gently with cold water. Drain well and transfer to an airtight container. Store in the fridge until required.

FOR THE CONFIT GOLDEN BEETROOT:

250 g baby golden beetroot, scrubbed and ends trimmed
200 ml olive oil
Sea salt
Black pepper

Heat the oven to 100°C. Put the baby beetroot in a small baking tray. Pour over the oil and season with salt and pepper. Cover with foil and cook for 1 ½–2 hours, or until cooked.

When cooked, rub off the skins with a clean cloth. Cut in half if small, or quarters if large.

FOR THE CONFIT MOKI:

500 g skinned moki fillet, cut into 4 × 125 g portions
Peel of 1 lemon
Olive oil
2 g Salt

Put two pieces of fish in a vacuum sealer bag. Add a drizzle of olive oil, a 1 cm piece of lemon peel and salt. Seal tightly and cook sous vide for 8–9 minutes (depending on thickness) at 68°C.

Open the bags and drain off any liquid. Pat the fish dry and serve.

TO ASSEMBLE:

Reserved small fennel fronds

Place a tablespoon of celeriac purée in the centre of four large plates. Top each with 3–4 pieces squid ink pasta. Arrange three pieces golden beetroot and three pieces pickled ice plant around the pasta, positioning them close to the purée. Gently place portions of confit moki on top of the pasta. Add 1 tablespoon of kuku sauce on each side of the fish. Pour 1 tablespoon of fishbone broth over the fish, then top with ½ tsp of yuzu caviar and a 1 cm fennel frond.

FRIED IKA COLLARS

SERVES 4

Fish collars are such an underutilised part of fish. Since Hiakai opened, we've done a variety of fish collar preparations for our snack menu. This version is a crowd favourite. The crunchiness of the skin and fins combined with the richness of the meat is a textural delight. Just pick them up and eat them with your hands.

FOR THE PIPI SEASONING:
3 g coriander seeds
2 g cumin seeds
20 g brown sugar
40 g sea salt
40 g Pipi Powder (see page 263)
Finely grated zest of 1 lemon

Toast the cumin and coriander until fragrant. Remove from the heat and grind into powder with the brown sugar. Stir in the other ingredients and taste for seasoning. Store in an airtight container until required.

FOR THE IKA (FISH) WINGS:
8 ika wings, cleaned, scaled and dried
200 g rice flour
50 g Nasturtium Vinegar (see page 252)
Pipi seasoning

Heat oil in a deep-fryer to 180°C. Dip the wings in rice flour, tapping to remove any excess. Deep-fry until golden and cooked through. Drain well in a mesh sieve, then spray to coat with Nasturtium Vinegar. Coat the wings in a generous amount of pipi seasoning. To serve, arrange large, clean pebbles on a plate and lay the wings on top. Serve immediately.

MANONO-CURED KAHAWAI

SERVES 4

Kahawai is an underrated fish. It has firm flesh and a high oil content which – when treated right – can be like butter in the mouth. The cure in this recipe adds a depth of earthiness to the kahawai, and the pickled melon adds a touch of acidity to cut through the richness of the cured fish.

FOR THE MANONO-CURED KAHAWAI:

10 g table salt
40 g sugar
15 g dried manono bark, finely ground
500 g kahawai fillet, skinned and boned

Put the salt, sugar and manono bark in a spice grinder and blend to a fine powder.

Line a tray with baking paper and arrange the kahawai on top. Rub the manono cure all over the fillets, then cover tightly with plastic wrap (pressed down in contact with the fish). Transfer to the fridge to cure for 48 hours, then hang the fillets in a well-ventilated 3°C fridge for 5 days.

FOR THE PICKLED ROCK MELON:

100 g sugar
10 g salt
200 ml white wine vinegar
¼ rock melon, peeled and deseeded

Put the sugar, salt and vinegar in a small pot set over medium heat. Bring to a simmer, stirring until the sugar and salt are dissolved. Remove from the heat and allow to cool.

Using a mandoline, shave the melon into 2 mm-thick ribbons (1 cm wide × 5 cm long). Drop the melon ribbons into the cooled liquid and leave them to pickle for 1 hour.

TO ASSEMBLE:

Lemon-infused olive oil

Slice the cured kahawai into 2 mm-thick pieces (about 4–5 cm long). Overlap two slices on each plate and add two loosely rolled pickled melon ribbons. Brush lightly with lemon olive oil and serve.

PĀUA SKEWERS WITH DARK BEER GLAZE

SERVES 4

At Hiakai, our menu starts with an ever-changing selection of rapid-fire snacks. Since opening, we've always done some form of skewer cooked over coals in our parilla grill. This pāua skewer, finished with a dark beer glaze, is one of our all-time favourites.

FOR THE DARK BEER GLAZE:
100 g honey
25 g glucose
50 g white wine vinegar
200 ml dark beer

Put all ingredients in a saucepan set over medium heat. Cook, stirring occasionally, until the mixture has reduced by three-quarters and has a thick, syrupy consistency. Set aside to cool, then transfer to an airtight container and store in the fridge until required.

FOR THE PAUA:
2 pāua, shucked, guts discarded
50 g olive oil
4 cloves garlic, peeled and sliced
15 ml lemon juice
1 dried manono leaf

Put all the ingredients in a vacuum bag and seal tightly. Cook sous vide at 75°C for 2½ hours, then allow to cool completely. Cut into 1.5–2 mm slices and slide them onto a skewer. Char over a coal barbecue and brush with beer glaze, then serve immediately on a warm plate.

TUNA, MARINATED HEIRLOOM TOMATOES, HOROPITO-TOMATO DASHI

SERVES 4

My friends Anthony and Angela Tringham grow the most delicious tomatoes in Aotearoa. Their heirloom tomatoes have the perfect balance of sweetness and acidity. Their tomatoes matched with the fattiness of tuna and spiciness of horopito make for a beautifully light and bright summery kaimoana course.

FOR THE HOROPITO-TOMATO DASHI:

250 g tomatoes, diced
1 bay leaf
2 g dried seaweed
½ kombu sheet
50 g parsley stalks
1 T vegetable oil
40 g red onion, peeled and diced
4 g garlic, peeled and finely sliced
2 g dried horopito flakes
1 g coriander seeds
1 g fennel seeds
80 ml white wine
2 L water
25 g mānuka honey
Freshly grated zest and juice of 1 lemon
Cayenne pepper
Salt
1 T cornflour, mixed with 1 T water

Put the tomatoes (and any trimmings), bay leaf, seaweed, kombu and parsley stalks in a large container and set aside.

Set a very large pot over medium heat and add the oil. Sauté the onion and garlic until soft, then stir in the horopito flakes, coriander seeds and fennel seeds. Cook for 2 minutes, then pour in the white wine. Cook until reduced by half. Add the water and bring to the boil, then remove from the heat. Pour this liquid over the tomatoes and allow to cool. Cover and store in the fridge for 24 hours.

The next day, strain the liquid into a large pot set over low heat. Let it reduce slowly and don't let it boil. Keep the tomato chunks for the tuna skin

crumb recipe (see page 186). When the liquid has reduced by three-quarters, remove from the heat and stir in the honey, lemon zest and juice. Add cayenne pepper and salt to taste. If necessary, whisk in a small amount of the cornflour mixture to adjust the texture.

FOR THE TUNA BALLOTINE:

1.2 kg tuna, skin on
4 nori sheets, cut in half
Flaky sea salt, to season

Skin and clean the tuna. Set the skin aside for the tuna skin crumb recipe. Cut each fillet into 3–4 pieces, depending on the size, and season with flaky sea salt. Wrap the tuna pieces in the nori and roll into a ballotine shape (use plastic wrap to make this easier). Vacuum-pack the tuna and cook in a steamer for 6–7 minutes. Remove from the steamer and plunge into a bowl of iced water to halt the cooking process. When ready to serve, unwrap the tuna and cut into ½ cm slices. Char on a barbecue for 1–2 minutes.

FOR THE MARINATED HEIRLOOM TOMATOES:
300 g beefsteak tomatoes
300 ml olive oil
3 g horopito flakes
200 g parsley, roughly chopped
½ bunch of thyme, leaves picked
Freshly grated zest and squeezed juice of 1 lemon
Salt
Mānuka wood chips

Use a blowtorch to remove the tomato skins, then cut the tomatoes into 2cm slices. Lay them on a rack set on a baking tray. Wrap with foil and smoke with mānuka chips. Repeat this process twice.

Put the oil, horopito, parsley, thyme, lemon zest and juice in a high-speed blender. Blend until combined and add salt to taste.

Transfer the smoked tomatoes to a shallow tray and pour over the oil and herb marinade. Leave to marinate for at least 6 hours. Remove the tomatoes from the marinade and cut into desired shapes.

FOR THE TUNA-SKIN CRUMB:
Tuna skin (reserved from tuna ballotine recipe above), stripped of excess meat or fat
Salt
10 g tomato pulp (reserved from the dashi)
100 g fresh breadcrumbs

Put the tuna skin in a small pot. Cover with cold water and add salt. Set over medium heat and bring to the boil, then remove from the heat and drain. Lay the skins on a dehydrator tray. Dry for 4 hours at 65°C. Put the tomato pulp on a dehydrator tray and dry for 4 hours at 65°C. Once dried, transfer to a high-speed blender and blend to a powder.

Deep-fry the dried skin at 320°C until very crisp. Season with a touch of salt and crush into pieces using the back of a knife. Stir the crispy tuna skin pieces and tomato powder into the breadcrumbs and season with salt. Store in an airtight container until required.

FOR THE KELP SALAD:
1 T sunflower oil
2 shallots, peeled and finely diced
50 ml Chardonnay vinegar
2 radishes, peeled and finely diced
100 g kelp, thinly sliced
Freshly grated zest and juice of 1 lemon
Olive oil
Salt, to taste

Set a small pan over medium heat. Add the oil, then sauté the shallots until soft. Deglaze with the Chardonnay vinegar. Once the vinegar has evaporated, add the radishes and remove from the heat. Tip into a bowl and add the kelp, lemon zest and juice, and a drizzle of olive oil. Season with salt to taste.

TO ASSEMBLE:
Micro mustard frill leaves
Red-veined sorrel

Heat a grill until very hot. Sear the tuna ballotine pieces, flesh side down, for 2 minutes. Turn over and cook for a further 2 minutes. The tuna should be hot in the middle.

Arrange the marinated heirloom tomatoes on four plates. Top each tomato with 1 tsp kelp salad. Place the tuna ballotine among the tomatoes and drizzle horopito-tomato dashi over everything. Finish the dish by topping each piece of tuna with ½ tsp tuna-skin crumbs. Garnish with micro mustard frill leaves and red-veined sorrel.

SLOW-ROASTED CABBAGE WITH TĪTĪ XO

SERVES 4

This dish is a tribute to Pawa, a soldier who travelled along Te Awa o Whanganui with Kupe but drowned while trying to collect kōrau (wild cabbage). I've spent a lot of time along Te Awa o Whanganui doing pop-ups. After heavy rain, the awa turns from jade to mud brown. We created a sauce to symbolise this with different textures of cabbage.

FOR THE SLOW-ROASTED CABBAGE:
1 whole white cabbage

Preheat the oven to 160°C. Put the whole cabbage in a baking tray and roast for 3–5 hours, until black and soft. Remove from the oven. Set a tray on top and add a heavy weight. Press overnight.

The next day, strain off the juices and reserve for the sauce. Cut the cabbage into four. Before serving, char each piece over a barbecue.

FOR THE TĪTĪ XO:
1 Confit Tītī (see page 250)
1 T sunflower oil
1 onion, peeled and diced
2 cloves garlic, finely chopped
3 fresh chillies, finely chopped
100 g dried green-lipped mussels
100 g dried pipi
½ T shrimp paste
100 g gluten-free soy sauce
100 g oyster sauce

Pull the meat off a confit tītī and chop it finely (using a knife or a food processor), ensuring there are no bones. Set aside.

Set a saucepan over medium heat. Add the sunflower oil, then the onion, garlic and chillies. Sauté until lightly caramelised. Stir in the tītī meat, mussels, pipi and shrimp paste, then pour in the soy and oyster sauces and cook over low heat until the dried shellfish are soft. Remove from the heat and purée in a food processor. Transfer to an airtight container and store in the fridge until required.

FOR THE CABBAGE SAUCE:
125 ml fresh cabbage juice (put half a white cabbage through a juicer)
All juices from the slow-roasted cabbage
125 ml chicken stock
10 g butter
10 g flour

Pour the fresh cabbage juice into a pot and simmer over medium heat for 2 minutes. Remove from the heat and filter through a muslin cloth.

Set a clean pot over medium heat. Add the butter and allow to melt, then add the flour, stirring with a wooden spoon to form a roux. Cook until golden, then whisk in the cabbage juices and stock. Cook, stirring constantly, for another 5 minutes or until the sauce is silky and creamy. Pass through a fine sieve and keep warm until ready to serve.

FOR THE PICKLED RED CABBAGE:
250 ml white wine vinegar
125 g caster sugar
12 g table salt
4 red cabbage leaves

Set a small pot over medium heat. Add the vinegar, sugar and salt, whisking to dissolve. Cut the cabbage leaves into rounds with a 3 cm cookie cutter and add to the pot. Remove from the heat and let cool to room temperature.

FOR THE CHICKEN CRUMBS:

50 g chicken skin
10 g butter
50 g breadcrumbs
¼ bunch chives, finely chopped

Heat the oven to 170°C. Line an oven tray with baking paper and lay the chicken skin on top. Bake for about 30 minutes, until golden and crunchy. Remove from the oven and allow to cool, then break into small pieces.

Melt the butter in a cast-iron pan until it caramelises. Add the breadcrumbs and toss through the butter until golden. Season with salt and transfer to a bowl. Once cool, add the chives and chopped chicken skin.

TO ASSEMBLE:

Baby kale leaves

Arrange a portion of charred cabbage on each plate. Cover the upward-facing side with tītī XO and sprinkle with chicken crumbs. Garnish with 3 baby kale leaves and 3 rounds cut out of each of the red cabbage leaves. Pour 2–3 tablespoons cabbage sauce on the side.

ROASTED TĪTĪ, TARO GRATIN, BRAISED PŪHĀ

SERVES 4

The Sunday Roast – a British tradition dating as far back as King Henry VII. Sunday is usually my one and only day off, and nine times out of ten I spend that day having some form of roast dinner with my whānau. Think of this as a Sunday Roast reimagined through a Māori-Sāmoan lens.

FOR THE TARO GRATIN:
2 kg taro, peeled, halved and cut into 2 mm slices
1 onion, peeled and thinly sliced
200 ml coconut cream
100 ml water
Salt
Pepper
1 T sunflower oil

Heat the oven to 160°C. Line a small baking tray (approx. 20 cm × 20 cm × 5 cm) with baking paper and set aside.

Put the taro, onion, coconut cream and water in a large bowl. Season with salt and pepper and mix well. Layer slices of the taro and onion in the tray, pouring some of the seasoned coconut cream between each layer. Cover tightly with baking paper and foil and bake for 1–1 ½ hours, until it yields easily to the point of a knife. Remove from the oven and put a tray the same size on top to weight it down. Allow to cool, then refrigerate overnight.

The next day, lift the gratin from the tray and cut into 10 cm × 20 cm rectangles. Set a non-stick pan over medium heat. Add the sunflower oil and sear the gratin portions on each side. Keep warm in a low oven until ready to serve.

FOR THE BRAISED PŪHĀ:
1 bunch pūhā, leaves picked (flowers and stems discarded)
1 T sunflower oil
1 clove garlic, peeled and finely chopped
200 ml chicken stock
Salt
Pepper

Wash the pūhā well then drain in a sieve, squeezing with your hands to remove any excess water. Chop roughly and set aside.

Set a pot over medium heat and add the oil. Sweat the garlic in the oil until fragrant, then add the pūhā and cook until soft. Pour in the chicken stock and lower the heat. Cook for at least 30 minutes, until very soft. Season to taste with salt and pepper and keep warm until ready to serve.

FOR THE ROASTED TĪTĪ:
1 tītī, gutted
4 sprigs rosemary
1 small bunch thyme
Flaky sea salt
Black pepper, freshly ground

Stuff the tītī with rosemary and thyme, then truss the bird with butcher's twine so the legs and wings are secured tightly to the body. Set the bird on a rack on a tray. Cook over low heat in a charcoal barbecue or in a 170°C oven for 35–40 minutes, turning to ensure the skin cooks evenly. Baste the bird with rendered fat during the cooking process. Allow to rest for 5 minutes before serving, carve the tītī and serve with pūhā and taro gratin.

WEKA WITH PUMPKIN & BOIL-UP BROTH

SERVES 6

There are a lot of rules and restrictions surrounding the hunting of weka (see page 110), which must be adhered to. I was given these birds as a koha from some friends on the Chatham Islands. Most people will not have access to weka, in which case duck or even chicken would make a suitable alternative.

FOR THE BRAISED WEKA:

3 whole weka
5 T vegetable oil
1 white onion, peeled and diced
1 carrot, peeled and diced
2 celery ribs, diced
3 cloves garlic
2 fresh horopito leaves
1 bay leaf
4 sprigs thyme
½ tsp black peppercorns
1.2 L chicken stock

Remove the legs and thighs from each bird, keeping the joints intact. Carefully remove and discard the skin. Set the legs and thighs aside at room temperature and reserve the carcasses for the broth.

Set a large stockpot over medium-hot heat. Once it's to temperature, add 2 T oil. Lightly sear the weka legs in batches, then set them aside at room temperature.

Return the pot to the heat and add the remaining oil, followed by the onion, carrot, celery and garlic. Cook them, stirring occasionally, until lightly caramelised. Add the horopito, bay leaf, thyme and black peppercorns. Stir well and cook for a further 2 minutes.

Return the weka legs to the pot and pour in the chicken stock. Stir to combine, and lower the heat to a gentle simmer. Cover with a cartouche (or a lid left slightly ajar) and cook for 3 hours, or until the meat is almost falling off the bone.

Once the weka legs are cooked, remove them from the braising liquid to serve. If not serving immediately, keep them in the braising liquid until needed.

FOR THE BOIL-UP BROTH:

2 kg pork bones
3 weka carcasses
5 T olive oil
2 large onions, peeled and chopped
2 large carrots, peeled and chopped
½ bunch celery, chopped
4 cloves garlic, smashed
3 L chicken stock
1 bunch thyme
2 fresh horopito leaves
1 T black peppercorns
½ marrow, deseeded and diced
1 bunch watercress, leaves picked and blanched
250 g baby spinach leaves, blanched
500 ml olive oil
Salt
Freshly squeezed lime juice, to season

Heat an oven to 180°C. Put the pork bones and weka carcasses into a baking dish and roast for 25–30 minutes, or until golden brown.

Set a large stockpot over medium heat. Add 2 tablespoons oil, followed by the onion, carrot, celery and garlic. Sauté until lightly caramelised, then add the roasted bones and carcasses. Pour in the chicken stock and add the thyme, horopito and peppercorns. Simmer for about 3 hours. Strain the stock and discard the bones and vegetables. Set the stock aside for the moment.

Set a clean stockpot over medium-hot heat. Once it's to temperature, add 3 tablespoons oil, followed by the marrow. Cook, stirring constantly, until very soft (don't let it burn on the bottom of the pot). When the marrow is almost cooked

through, pour in the stock and simmer gently for
20 minutes. Remove from the heat and blend in
batches in a high-speed blender or Thermomix,
adding the blanched watercress, baby spinach and
olive oil as you go. The soup should emulsify as you
blend it, becoming very silky and bright green. Pass
the soup through a fine chinois or fine mesh sieve,
and season with salt and lime juice. Serve hot.

FOR THE ROASTED PUMPKIN:

1 butternut pumpkin, peeled, halved lengthwise and
    deseeded
2 kūmara, peeled and cut into 2 cm dice
Olive oil
Flaky sea salt
Dried horopito flakes

Heat the oven to 160°C. Line an oven tray with
baking paper and grease lightly. Cut the butternut
into 2 cm-thick wedges (about 6–8 cm long). They
should be roughly the same size so they cook
evenly.

 Lay the butternut and kūmara on the prepared
tray and drizzle with a little olive oil. Sprinkle with
flaky sea salt and dried horopito flakes.

 Bake for 15–20 minutes, turning the pieces
periodically so they cook evenly. Remove from
the oven and serve immediately or at room
temperature.

TO ASSEMBLE:

Place one braised weka leg in each bowl and
arrange the roasted butternut and kūmara around
it. Garnish with a few picked watercress leaves and
pour the hot boil-up broth into the bowl. Serve
immediately.

BRAISED BRISKET, KAWAKAWA PURÉE, PICKLED KAREAO

SERVES 4

For this dish I wanted to pay homage to my late grandfather. Richard Hurunui grew up in Pātea, a small town not far from the base of Taranaki Maunga. At 15 he began working at the Pātea Freezing Works as a butcher. As a nod to this time, I developed a dish where the meat is slowly cooked with ngā tipu found around the base of the maunga.

FOR THE BRAISED BRISKET:

1 kg brisket

1 T vegetable oil

2 carrots, peeled and diced

1 onion, peeled and diced

1 celery stalk, washed and diced

1 leek, washed and diced

2 cloves garlic, peeled

5 fresh manono leaves

100 g fresh manono bark

½ bunch fresh thyme

½ bunch fresh rosemary

1 bouquet garni (1 cinnamon stick, 1 star anise,
    ½ tsp peppercorns)

10 g Dutch cocoa powder

50 ml red wine

2 L chicken stock

1 marrow bone, roasted

Cabernet Sauvignon vinegar

Flaky sea salt

Brown rice syrup

Heat the oven to 160°C.

Season the brisket with salt. Set aside for 30 minutes to dry-brine. Meanwhile, begin making the braise liquid. Set a large stockpot over medium heat and add the oil. When it's to temperature, add the carrots, onion, celery, leek and garlic. Cook, stirring occasionally, until all the vegetables are a deep golden caramel colour. Add the manono leaves and bark, thyme, rosemary, bouquet garni and cocoa. Cook for 1 minute, stirring continuously so the cocoa doesn't burn. Pour in the red wine, stirring vigorously until the liquid has evaporated. Pour in the chicken stock and stir well. Add in the marrow bone and simmer for 10 minutes.

Set a heavy pan over high heat. Sear the brisket on all sides in a little oil, then transfer to a large, deep oven dish. Pour the braising liquid over the brisket. Cover tightly with baking paper and foil. Cook in the oven for 3½–4 hours, then remove from the oven. Lift the brisket from the braising liquid and allow to cool completely before slicing.

Strain the liquid through a fine sieve into a large stockpot. Keep half the liquid for reheating the brisket. Pour the remainder into a pot and simmer over low heat until it reaches a jus consistency. Season the jus to taste with Cabernet Sauvignon vinegar, salt and brown rice syrup.

FOR THE KAWAKAWA PURÉE:

1 T baking soda
70 g kawakawa leaves
20 g fresh parsley
1 kg zucchini, peeled (keep the skins), halved lengthwise
 and sliced 3 mm thick
1 T sunflower oil
1 clove garlic, peeled and sliced 2 mm thick
Xanthan gum
Flaky sea salt

Bring 2 litres of water to the boil over medium heat and add the baking soda. Blanch the kawakawa leaves until they are mushy but remain bright green. Remove with a slotted spoon and plunge into a bowl of iced water. Transfer the leaves to a fine sieve, then wrap in cheesecloth and squeeze out the excess water.

Repeat this blanching, cooling and draining process with the parsley and zucchini skins. Set them all aside.

Set a large pan over medium heat and add the sunflower oil. Sauté the garlic until fragrant, then add the sliced zucchini and cook until soft.

Tip the cooked zucchini and garlic mixture into a high-speed blender, along with the blanched skins and leaves. Purée until smooth. Add 1.5 g xanthan gum per 1 litre of purée to stabilise it. Season with flaky sea salt and pass through a fine sieve.

FOR THE SLOW-COOKED ONIONS:

200 g small brown onions, peeled and halved lengthwise
Vegetable oil
Sea salt

Put the onions into vacuum bags. Drizzle with oil and season with salt, then seal tightly. Cook sous vide for 1 hour at 90°C, until the onions are soft and cooked through. Remove from the bag and drain.

Set a heavy pan over high heat. Sear the onions, cut side down, until deep golden brown. Remove from the pan and carefully pull apart the layers. Serve immediately.

FOR THE BONE MARROW CRUMB:

1 marrow bone
50 g thyme leaves, chopped
100 g breadcrumbs

Heat the oven to 180°C. Put the marrow bone in a small pan and roast for 30 minutes. Pour off and retain the fat, and keep the bone for the brisket braising liquid (see recipe above).

Pour the fat into a small pan set over medium heat. Add the thyme and breadcrumbs, stirring until the crumbs are golden and crisp. Remove from the heat and allow to cool, then store in an airtight container.

TO ASSEMBLE:

5–6 pieces pickled kareao per person
3–4 watercress leaves per person

Bring the reserved braising liquid up to a simmer. Place the brisket in the liquid and warm for 45 minutes.

Place a large spoonful of kawakawa purée on each plate, spreading it in a half-moon shape with an offset spatula. Place one portion of brisket on each plate and top with bone marrow crumbs, pickled kareao, watercress and slow-cooked onions.

PORK BELLY, KĀNGA KŌPIRO, CABBAGE, PLUM JUS

SERVES 12

My old apartment in New York didn't have much going for it. The only upside was an amazing bakery serving 'DIY Grits' across the road. When I moved out, those grits were the only thing I missed. Consider this dish a tribute to the humble cups of 'DIY Grits' from my former years.

FOR THE CONFIT PORK BELLY:

1 T cumin seeds, toasted
1 T fennel seeds, toasted
2 g freshly ground black pepper
3 large cloves garlic, peeled and thinly sliced
10 g flaky sea salt
1.5 kg pork belly, skin on, bone out
3 L melted pork fat

Combine the spices, garlic and salt. Rub all over the pork belly, then lay it on a rack set on a tray. Leave to cure in the fridge overnight.

The next day, wipe the cure from the meat. Heat the oven to 120°C. Put the pork belly, skin-side down, in a large, deep oven dish. Pour over the melted pork fat. Cover the dish tightly with foil and cook for about 3 hours, or until the meat is very tender.

Remove from the oven and leave to cool at room temperature for 30 minutes. Carefully lift the pork belly out of the fat and transfer to a baking-paper-lined tray. Set another tray on top of the meat and weight it down with a few large tins or a heavy frying pan. Leave overnight in the fridge. The next day, slice into 100 g pieces.

To serve, heat the oven to 170°C. Season the skin side of the pork belly with flaky sea salt. Put the pork belly, skin-side down, on a cast-iron skillet and transfer to the oven for 10–12 minutes. Once the skin is deep golden and crispy, flip the pork belly over and cook for another 3–4 minutes. Remove from the oven and serve immediately.

FOR THE KANGA KOPIRO:

250 g kānga kōpiro corn kernels (see page 63)
2 T vegetable oil
1 white onion, peeled and finely diced
2 garlic cloves, finely chopped
200 ml cream
300–400 ml white chicken stock
100 g unsalted butter
Salt, to taste
Black pepper, freshly ground, to taste

Grind the kānga kōpiro corn kernels using a meat grinder. Repeat this process to ensure each kernel has been sufficiently broken down.

Set a saucepan over medium heat. Add the oil, followed by the onion. Cook until the onion is soft and translucent, then stir in the garlic. Cook until the garlic has started to soften, then tip in the ground kānga kōpiro corn and stir well. Keep stirring and slowly add the cream and chicken stock. Stir continuously to prevent the kānga kōpiro from catching on the bottom. The mixture should resemble creamy polenta or grits. If it needs more liquid, add more white chicken stock. If the mixture becomes too runny, lower the heat and cook slowly until some of the liquid has reduced. Once the consistency is right, stir in the butter and season to taste with salt and black pepper. Stir well and serve immediately.

FOR THE CABBAGE:

2 T vegetable oil
½ white cabbage, finely shredded
2 shallots, peeled and thinly sliced
100 ml white chicken stock
1 small bunch chives, finely shredded
1 small bunch parsley, finely shredded
100 ml Chardonnay vinegar
1–2 T olive oil
Flaky sea salt

Line a tray with paper towels and set aside.

Set a sauté pan over high heat. Add the vegetable oil, followed by the cabbage and shallots. Toss until the vegetables start to wilt and soften, then pour in the chicken stock to deglaze the pan. Toss again, then tip the vegetables onto the prepared tray. Leave to cool to room temperature.

Transfer the cooled cabbage to a bowl. Stir through the chives, parsley and Chardonnay vinegar. Drizzle with 1–2 tablespoons of olive oil and season with flaky sea salt. Serve immediately at room temperature or warmed.

FOR THE PLUM JUS:

3 kg chicken bones
2 onions, peeled and diced
2 carrots, peeled and diced
½ bunch celery, peeled and diced
½ bulb garlic
4 sprigs rosemary
2 bunches thyme
3 very ripe Black Doris plums, pitted and chopped
Plum vinegar
Flaky sea salt

Preheat the oven to 200°C. Spread the chicken bones in an oven tray. Roast until evenly dark golden brown. Transfer the roasted bones to a large stockpot. Add the vegetables and herbs and cover with cold water. Bring to a simmer and cook over low heat for 8 hours.

The next day, strain the stock and return the liquid to the pot. Cook over low-medium heat until reduced by half. Add the plums and continue to cook the stock gently until it's one-third its original volume. Pass through a fine sieve and season to taste with plum vinegar and flaky sea salt.

TO ASSEMBLE:

Put one portion of pork belly on each plate and spoon 3 tablespoons of hot kānga kōpiro alongside. Garnish with a small mound of pickled cabbage and a drizzle of plum jus.

SWEET

KAWAKAWA SORBET, LIME MERINGUE

SERVES 4

What struck me about kawakawa when I first tried it was how refreshing it is. I knew almost immediately that I wanted to create a sorbet using the leaves. I've done multiple desserts involving kawakawa, but I love the simplicity of this one, allowing the diner to experience the peppery freshness of kawakawa in full force.

FOR THE LIME GEL:

75 ml fresh lime juice
Zest of the juiced lime
300 ml Simple Syrup (see page 252)
3 g agar

Put the lime juice, zest, 200 ml of the Simple Syrup and the agar in a small pot set over medium heat. Bring to a simmer and cook for 5 minutes, stirring constantly. Remove from the heat and pour through a fine sieve into a bowl. Chill for 4 hours or until set.

When set, cut the gel into cubes and transfer to a blender. Start blending at low speed, then gradually increase the speed to medium. Pour in the remaining Simple Syrup 30 ml at a time, to help obtain a silky texture. The gel should be firm enough to hold a peak.

FOR THE LIME MERINGUE:

2 egg whites
90 g caster sugar
2 limes

Line a dehydrator tray with baking paper and set aside.

Put the egg whites into the bowl of a stand mixer. Start whisking them at medium speed. Once fluffy and white, slowly add the sugar. Whisk until the meringue holds firmly. Transfer to a piping bag fitted with a small pastry nozzle. Pipe 5 mm dots on the lined tray. Using a microplane, shower lime zest over the meringue dots. Dry overnight at 65°C. Store in an airtight container until needed.

FOR THE WHIPPED YOGHURT:

100 g plain Greek yoghurt
10 g icing sugar

Whisk the yoghurt and icing sugar together until smooth. Transfer to a piping bag and store in the fridge until required.

FOR THE KAWAKAWA ESSENCE:

1 T baking soda
40 g fresh kawakawa leaves
150 ml Simple Syrup (see page 252)

Bring 1 L of water to a boil. Sprinkle in the baking soda, then add the kawakawa leaves. Blanch the leaves until they are mushy but remain bright green. Transfer the leaves immediately to an ice bath to stop the cooking process. Drain in a sieve, then wrap in cheesecloth and squeeze out the excess water.

Put the blanched leaves and Simple Syrup in a blender and blend for 30 seconds, or until the leaves have completely dissolved. Strain through cheesecloth into a bottle and store in the fridge until required.

FOR THE KAWAKAWA SORBET:

1 T baking soda
60 g fresh kawakawa leaves
3 Granny Smith apples, skin on
5 limes, zest and juice
75 g spinach juice
500 ml Simple Syrup (see page 252)
2 g xanthan gum

Bring 1 litre of water to a boil. Sprinkle in the baking soda, then add the kawakawa leaves. Blanch the leaves until they are mushy but remain bright green. Transfer the leaves immediately to an ice bath to stop the cooking process. Drain in a sieve, then wrap in cheesecloth and squeeze out the excess water.

Core and dice one apple, then freeze. Juice the remaining apples. Transfer the juice to a blender and add the lime juice and zest, the blanched kawakawa leaves and the Simple Syrup. Add the frozen apple, xanthan gum and spinach juice. Start blending on low speed, then gradually increase the speed to high for 1 minute. Pass through a fine sieve. You'll need a refractometer for sorbet making, if you don't have one then you'll just have to churn it and hope for the best. If you do have a refractometer, use it now to check that the sugar level is between 18 to 20 nD. Add more lime juice to adjust the sugar level if required. Transfer to an ice-cream maker and churn until frozen. Store in an airtight container in the fridge.

TO ASSEMBLE:

Put nine small dots of lime gel and nine small dots of whipped yoghurt in the centre of four small bowls. Crush three lime meringues with your fingers and sprinkle over the lime gel. Top each bowl with a quenelle of kawakawa sorbet and finish with a teaspoon of kawakawa essence.

KIEKIE, STRAWBERRY, RHUBARB SORBET

SERVES 4

This was the first pre-dessert we ever served at the restaurant. The winter before we opened, we collected kiekie blossoms and infused half into gin and the other half into Simple Syrup (see page 252). After months of steeping, our jars of Kiekie Gin and syrup were ready to use and this was the resulting dish.

FOR THE RHUBARB SORBET:
1 bunch (5 sticks) rhubarb, washed and diced
300 ml water
70 g sugar
30 g glucose
4 g citric acid

Put the rhubarb in a medium saucepan and cover with water. Set over medium heat and cook until the rhubarb is completely soft. Purée, then transfer to an airtight container and chill until required.

Put the 300ml water and sugar in a small saucepan set over medium heat. Bring to a simmer, then stir in the glucose. Remove from the heat and allow to cool. Add 330 g rhubarb purée and the citric acid to the pot, then mix thoroughly with a stick blender. Transfer to an ice-cream maker and churn until frozen. Store in an airtight container in the freezer.

FOR THE KIEKIE STRAWBERRIES:
4 strawberries, hulled and cut into 2 mm slices
9 g Simple Syrup (see page 252)
9 g Kiekie Gin (see page 254)

Put the sliced strawberries in a small bowl. Pour over the syrup and gin and leave to marinate for at least 2 hours.

FOR THE KIEKIE JELLY SHEETS:
150 g Kiekie Gin (see page 254)
1.5 g agar

Put the gin in a small pot set over medium heat. Bring to a simmer and add the agar. Cook for 4 minutes, stirring constantly. Remove from the heat and pour over a flat tray (the mixture should be paper-thin). Leave to set in the fridge for about 1 hour. Cut into 4 cm × 4 cm squares when ready to serve.

FOR THE STRAWBERRY EXTRACT:
4 strawberries, hulled and cut into small dice
2 g lemon juice
2 g icing sugar

Put all the ingredients in a small bowl and leave to infuse overnight in the fridge.

TO ASSEMBLE:
Rose petals

Put three kiekie strawberry slices in each bowl. Top with a quenelle of rhubarb sorbet. Sprinkle with 4–5 drops of strawberry extract and balance a kiekie jelly sheet on top. Sprinkle with rose petals.

MANONO-POACHED PEARS, HOROPITO ICE CREAM, ALMOND SOIL

SERVES 8

The flavour and colour that can be extracted from manono bark lends itself beautifully to both sweet and savoury applications. The pears in this recipe are best made a day in advance and left to soak in the manono syrup overnight.

FOR THE HOROPITO ICE CREAM:
180 ml milk
180 ml cream
4 egg yolks
45 g sugar
1 T dried horopito leaves (see page 262)
Pinch of sea salt

Combine the milk and cream in a saucepan set over medium heat. Bring to a simmer, stirring occasionally, then remove from the heat.

Whisk the egg yolks and sugar until creamy. Keep stirring and slowly pour in the warm milk mixture (don't rush or you may scramble the eggs). Pour the combined mixture into a clean saucepan and set over low-medium heat. Cook, stirring constantly, until the custard is thick enough to coat the back of a spoon.

Remove from the heat and add the dried horopito and salt. Transfer to a covered container and chill overnight.

The next day, churn the custard in an ice-cream maker until set. It can be used immediately or stored in the freezer until required.

FOR THE ALMOND SOIL:
50 g plain sweet biscuits
50 g toasted almonds

Using a food processor, pulse the biscuits and almonds together until they resemble fine biscuit crumbs. Transfer to an airtight container and store in the fridge until required.

FOR THE MANONO-POACHED PEARS:
2 pears, peeled
20 g manono bark
1 L water
250 g sugar
2 star anise
30 ml Poire Williams liqueur
20 ml lemon juice

Put all the ingredients in a saucepan that's just big enough to hold the pears. The pears should be completely covered by the cooking liquid. Cover the pears with a baking paper cartouche (or a lid left slightly ajar). Set the saucepan over medium heat and bring to a gentle simmer. Cook for 1 hour or until cooked through. Don't allow the pears to boil or they will become mushy. Remove from the heat and allow the pears to cool in the liquid.

FOR THE PEAR GASTRIQUE:
300 ml manono-pear poaching liquid
150 ml apple cider vinegar
30 g mānuka honey

Combine all ingredients in a small saucepan set over low heat. Cook until the mixture has reduced by half. Remove from the heat and allow to cool. Serve at room temperature.

TO ASSEMBLE:
Core the pears and cut into quarters lengthwise. Spoon 2 T almond soil on the base of each bowl. Top with a pear quarter. Position a quenelle of horopito ice cream beside the pear and drizzle with 1–2 tsp pear gastrique. Garnish with edible flowers.

MĀNUKA HONEY CLOUD, MILK CRUMBS, WHIPPED GOAT'S CHEESE

SERVES 4

A dessert inspired by Kupe's wife Kuramārōtini, who upon noticing clouds on the horizon exclaimed, *He Ao! He Ao! He Aotearoa!* (A cloud! A cloud! A long white cloud!), thus giving our country its name.

FOR THE MILK CRUMBS:
80 g unsalted butter
60 g skim milk powder
3 g nutritional yeast flakes

Melt the butter in a large pan over medium heat, until it starts to foam. Slowly stir in the milk powder. Raise the heat to medium-high and shake the mixture (using a wooden spoon) until the milk powder is cooked and golden brown (you should see crumbs forming).

Tip the mixture into a cheesecloth-lined sieve to strain out the excess butter. Line a small tray with cheesecloth and spread the crumbs evenly on top. Freeze overnight.

When frozen solid, tip the mixture into a food processor fitted with a blade attachment and pulse into crumbs. Season with yeast flakes. Transfer to an airtight container and store in the fridge until required.

FOR THE GOAT'S CHEESE CURD:
20 ml cream
10 g fresh ginger, peeled and sliced
170 g goat's cheese curd
Table salt, to taste

Put the cream and ginger in a small pot. Bring to the boil over medium heat, then remove from the heat and leave to infuse for 5 minutes.

Put the goat's cheese in a bowl and mix with a rubber spatula. Strain the infused ginger cream over the top and mix well. Season with salt. Cover and store in the fridge until required.

FOR THE GOAT'S CHEESE MOUSSE:
50 ml milk
150 ml cream
20 g egg yolk
20 g caster sugar
75 g goat's cheese curd
2 x CO_2 chargers

Put the milk and cream in a small pot over medium heat. Warm until it reaches 65°C. Whisk the yolk and sugar until the sugar is fully incorporated. Slowly pour one-third of the hot cream into the egg mixture, whisking constantly. Whisk in the remaining cream, then return the mixture to the pot. Heat until it reaches 85°C. Put the curd in a bowl. Pour the custard through a sieve into the bowl, then stir to mix. Cover and chill. Put the mixture into a medium soda syphon and charge with two CO_2 cartridges. Shake well and refrigerate.

FOR THE MĀNUKA HONEY FOAM:
200 g mānuka honey
200 ml water
1 g table salt

Put all the ingredients in a blender and blend at medium speed for 45 seconds. Put the mixture into a medium soda syphon and charge with two CO_2 cartridges. Shake well and refrigerate until required.

TO ASSEMBLE:
Put 1 T of milk crumbs on each plate and top with a small quenelle of whipped goat's cheese. Cover each one with about 2 T goat's cheese mousse. Finish with a large spoon of mānuka honey foam.

MŌKEHU CURD, KIKORANGI, RĒWENA CRISPS

SERVES 4

You wouldn't think it to look at it, but mōkehu tastes a lot like almond. This was one of the first cheese courses we ever served at Hiakai. By infusing the mōkehu into milk, we were able to make a light curd that paired well with blue cheese and thyme, while the rēwena crisps add a bit of crunch.

FOR THE MOKEHU CURD:

240 ml milk
30 g fresh mokehu
Pinch of table salt
2 g agar

Put the milk in a small pot and bring to the boil over medium heat. Remove from the heat and add the mōkehu. Let it steep for 30 minutes, then pour the milk through a sieve (discard the mōkehu) and return it to the pot. Add the agar and cook over medium heat for 5 minutes, stirring constantly. Pour into a container and let it set overnight in the fridge.

The next day, cut the curd into small pieces and put it in a blender. Blend until smooth then transfer to a piping bag.

FOR THE REWENA CRISPS:

100 g rēwena breadcrumbs
50 g isomalt
2 g table salt

Heat the oven to 160°C (fan bake). Line a small oven tray with a silicone mat or baking paper.

Mix all the ingredients until well combined and tip into a fine sieve. Shake the sieve over the prepared tray – to form a 1–2 mm-thick layer of mixture. Bake for 8 minutes, or until golden. Cool, then transfer to an airtight container and store at room temperature.

TO ASSEMBLE:

2 T crumbled Kikorangi blue cheese
Lemon-infused olive oil
2 tsp lemon thyme leaves

Pipe about 12 to 15 small dots of mōkehu curd into each bowl. Scatter over the blue cheese. Break the rēwena tuile into small shards and sprinkle across the bowls. Finish with a few drops of the lemon-infused olive oil and a few leaves of lemon thyme.

RED MATIPO SORBET, APPLE CRISP, APPLE CREAMING SODA

SERVES 4

It took over a year of trial and error for us to figure out how to use red matipo. The leaves smell and taste subtly of crisp apple, but are so fibrous you wouldn't want to eat them straight from the shrub. When we finally extracted the flavour we were over the moon and immediately got to work on creating a dish with our new discovery.

FOR THE LEMON SUGAR:
4 lemons
300 g caster sugar
50 ml water

Peel the lemons, removing any white pith. Keep the lemon flesh for the red matipo sorbet.

Put the lemon peel in a small pot set over medium heat. Cover with cold water, then bring to the boil. Remove from the heat and strain the peel. Repeat this process three more times to remove any bitterness.

Return the blanched peel to the pot with 100 g of the sugar and 50 ml water. Cook until it reaches 150°C, then remove from the heat and add the remaining 200 g sugar. Shake the pot until the sugar crystallises. Pour onto a baking-paper-lined tray and allow to cool.

When cold, grind the lemon and sugar mixture in a blender until it becomes a fine powder. Transfer to an airtight container and store in a cool, dark place.

FOR THE RED MATIPO SORBET:
300 ml Red Matipo Syrup (see page 254)
250 ml water
30 ml Granny Smith apple juice
30 ml lemon juice
30 ml chickpea brine (aquafaba), chilled
1 g xanthan gum

Mix together the Red Matipo Syrup, water and fruit juices. Set aside.

Whisk the chickpea brine until light and fluffy, then whisk in the xanthan gum until it's thoroughly mixed. Pour into the syrup and blend with a stick blender. If you have a refractometer, use it now to check that the sugar level is at 21 nD. Readjust the sugar levels if required by adding a little more Red Matipo Syrup. Churn in an ice-cream machine, then transfer to an airtight container and store in the freezer.

FOR THE APPLE CREAMING SODA:

170 g (2) Granny Smith apples, cored
100 g caster sugar
4 g leaf gelatin, bloomed in cold
    water
2 egg whites
7 g citric acid
2 x CO_2 chargers

Juice the apples then pass the liquid through a fine sieve to remove any fibres. Pour into a small pot and set over low heat. Add the sugar and stir until it dissolves, then add the leaf gelatin. Stir until the gelatin has melted, then remove from the heat. Drain the leaf gelatin and squeeze out excess moisture.

Let cool slightly, then stir in the egg whites and citric acid. Pass through a fine sieve into a clean container and leave to set completely in the fridge.

Once set, pour into a soda syphon and charge with 2 CO_2 chargers. Make sure the syphon is fully charged and shaken well at least 1 hour before serving or the foam will not hold its shape.

FOR THE APPLE CRISP:

Freshly squeezed juice of ½ lemon
1 Granny Smith apple
250 ml Simple Syrup (see page 252)
1 g citric acid

Line a dehydrator tray with baking paper and set aside.

Pour the lemon juice and 250 ml water into a small bowl. Use a mandoline to cut the apple in 2 mm slices, starting from the bottom. Trim each slice into a circle using a 6 cm cookie cutter, then place in the lemon water to prevent them going brown.

Pour the Simple Syrup into a small pot and add the citric acid. Bring to a simmer over medium heat. Dip each apple slice in the simmering syrup for 20–30 seconds, until slightly soft and translucent, then lay them on the prepared dehydrator tray. Dry the apple slices for 90 minutes at 70°C, then turn them over and dry for another 90 minutes. Let the slices cool completely and firm up, then store in an airtight container at room temperature.

TO ASSEMBLE:

Tarata Gin (see page 256)

Put a teaspoonful of lemon sugar in the centre of four small bowls. Top with a quenelle of red matipo sorbet. Sprinkle each sorbet with 3–4 drops of Tarata Gin. Place a 2 cm × 2 cm spoon of creaming soda on the side of the sorbet (the peak of the creaming soda should be the same height as the sorbet) and top with an apple crisp.

KŪMARA ROROI WITH VANILLA ICE CREAM

SERVES 4

Roroi is the only Māori pudding known to have existed. We've never served this at the restaurant, but it's one of my favourite desserts for its simplicity and comfort. Traditionally it's made with new-season kūmara, which is when the vegetable is at its sweetest.

FOR THE KUMARA ROROI:

40 g butter
100 g caster sugar
50 g coconut sugar
600 g new-season kūmara, peeled and grated
¼ tsp nutmeg, freshly grated
¼ tsp cinnamon, ground

Heat the oven to 170°C. Grease a shallow baking dish with the butter and line with baking paper. Combine the sugars, then sprinkle half of the sugar over the bottom of the dish and the kūmara. Toss together the kūmara and spices, then pack firmly on top of the sugar. Sprinkle the remaining sugar on top. Cover with foil and bake for 1 hour. Remove the foil and bake for another 10 minutes.

FOR THE VANILLA ICE CREAM:

180 ml milk
180 ml cream
4 egg yolks
45 g sugar
½ vanilla bean, scraped for seeds
Pinch of sea salt

Combine the milk and cream in a saucepan set over medium heat. Bring to a simmer, stirring occasionally, then remove from the heat.

Whisk the egg yolks and sugar until creamy. Keep stirring and slowly pour in the warm milk mixture (don't rush or you may scramble the eggs). Pour the combined mixture into a clean saucepan and set over low-medium heat. Cook, stirring constantly, until the custard is thick enough to coat the back of a spoon.

Remove from the heat and add the vanilla bean seeds and salt. Transfer to a covered container and chill overnight.

The next day, churn the custard in an ice-cream maker until set. It can be used immediately or stored in the freezer until required.

TO ASSEMBLE:

Divide the roroi into four portions. Arrange each on a plate and top with a quenelle of vanilla ice cream. Serve immediately.

PETITS FOURS

HOROPITO BONBONS

MAKES ABOUT 60 FILLED CHOCOLATES

Horopito and chocolate is one of my favourite flavour combinations. Because I love combining food with art, I designed the outer shell to look like the green and crimson speckling of a horopito leaf. These bonbons have earned such a reputation that we receive special requests from people wanting to order them by the hundreds.

FOR THE HOROPITO CARAMEL:

250 g sugar
30 ml water
100 g unsalted butter, cut into ½ cm dice
5 g dried horopito leaves, flaked (see page 262)
150 g double cream
25 g milk chocolate
8 g sea salt

Put the sugar and 30 ml water in a pot set over medium heat. Cook until the sugar has caramelised to an amber colour (about 170°C). Remove from the heat and slowly stir in the butter using a wooden spoon. Add the horopito flakes.

Slowly pour in the cream, stirring constantly. If the caramel begins to set, return it to the heat for a few seconds.

Once the cream is incorporated, add the milk chocolate and sea salt. Blend with a stick blender until the mixture is smooth. Cool, then transfer to an airtight container and store in the fridge.

FOR THE COCOA BUTTER DECORATION:

100 g cocoa butter, divided into two 50 g amounts
200 g white chocolate, divided into four 50 g amounts
5 g red fat-soluble food colouring
5 g green fat-soluble food colouring

Start with the cocoa butter decoration. Put 50 g cocoa butter, 50 g white chocolate and the red colouring in a small metal bowl. Melt together in a double-boiler until the mixture reaches 45°C. Remove from the heat and slowly stir in another 50 g white chocolate. Keep stirring until the mixture reaches 29°C. Polish two 30 cm x 2 cm demisphere chocolate moulds with a soft cloth (this ensures the finished chocolates have a shiny surface). Using a small brush, flick the red chocolate mixture over the moulds. Let it set completely.

While you're waiting, make the green coating. Put the remaining 50 g cocoa butter, 50 g white chocolate and the green colouring in a small metal bowl. Melt together in a double-boiler until the mixture reaches 45°C. Remove from the heat and slowly stir in the remaining 50 g white chocolate. Keep stirring until the mixture reaches 29°C. Brush this green chocolate over the chocolate moulds and leave to set completely.

FOR THE TEMPERED CHOCOLATE SHELLS:
600 g dark chocolate (ideally, 64% cacao)

Temper the chocolate before you finish the shells.

Melt 450 g of the dark chocolate in a double-boiler set over low heat. Once it reaches 55°C, remove from the heat and slowly stir in the remaining 150 g dark chocolate using a rubber spatula. Stir until the mixture reaches 31°C. Pour the chocolate over the moulds, tapping the moulds and using a large metal spatula to remove any excess. Leave to set at room temperature. Transfer any remaining melted chocolate to a clean bowl and keep warm.

TO ASSEMBLE:
Once the moulds have set, fill each chocolate shell with the horopito caramel. Pour the remaining melted chocolate over the top, using a large metal spatula to remove the excess. Leave the chocolates in the fridge to set firmly, so you can pop them out of the moulds. Store in an airtight container in the fridge.

KAWAKAWA SHREWSBURY

MAKES ABOUT 15 FILLED COOKIES

A little something from my childhood with an indigenous kick.

FOR THE KAWAKAWA BERRY SABLÉ:
125 g plain flour
50 g icing sugar
5 g kawakawa berries, powdered (see page 262)
Pinch of table salt
90 g butter
1 egg yolk

Sift together the flour, icing sugar, kawakawa berry powder and salt. Rub in the butter until the mixture resembles breadcrumbs, then add the egg yolk and mix to a smooth dough. Roll out on a lined tray to 3 mm thick. Chill overnight.

Heat the oven to 160°C. Use a 2.5 cm round biscuit cutter to cut the dough into shapes and transfer them to a lined baking tray. If you have a small heart-shaped cutter, use this to cut a shape from the centre of half of the rounds. Leave to rest in the fridge for 30 minutes, then transfer to the oven and bake for 8–10 minutes, or until light golden. Transfer to a rack and allow to cool completely.

FOR THE SHREWSBURY JAM:
125 g sugar
20 g glucose
15 g water
50 g fresh raspberries

Put all the ingredients in a small pot and set it over medium heat. Stir with a wooden spoon and cook until the mixture reaches 130°C. Transfer to a metal bowl and allow to cool before using. The jam should be very thick and sticky.

TO ASSEMBLE:
Sandwich the biscuits together with a small blob of jam (making sure the biscuits with the heart-shaped cut-outs are on top). Store in an airtight container.

MAMAKU PÂTE DE FRUIT

MAKES 150 CUBES

This petit four came into existence by accident. I'd been attempting to make a tarte tatin using mamaku as a replacement for apple – it tasted okay, but was a gluey mess. I put the failed tart in the fridge and decided to give it another go in the morning. When I returned the next day, the 'slime' had solidified into a firm jelly.

FOR THE MAMAKU PURÉE:
300 g mamaku frond, cleaned under cold running water
200 ml water

Peel the mamaku frond with a small, sharp knife. Discard the outer skin and cut the flesh into 5 mm slices. Put the mamaku and water in a small pot set over medium heat. Cook until you can easily run a knife through it, then remove from the heat. Transfer the mamaku and cooking water into a blender or food processor. Blend until it forms a purée. Pass through a fine sieve and divide into 100 g portions. You need 100 g for the following recipe; any excess can be frozen in a covered container.

FOR THE PÂTE DE FRUIT:
100 g mamaku purée
210 ml water
15 g glucose
215 g white sugar
8 g pectin powder
5 g tartaric acid

Use baking spray to grease a 15 cm × 15 cm heatproof baking dish.

Put the mamaku purée, water and glucose in a medium pot. Bring to a boil.

Thoroughly mix the sugar and pectin powder (it is crucial to avoid lumps) and add to the boiling mamaku mixture. Cook until it reaches 107°C on a thermometer, whisking constantly to avoid unwanted caramelisation at the bottom of the pot.

Dissolve the tartaric acid in 10 ml water. Whisk into the pot for no more than 10 seconds, then pour the mixture into the prepared dish. Let it cool completely. Once set, cut into 150 small cubes and store in a covered container in the fridge.

FOR THE FIZZY SUGAR:
50 g caster sugar
1 g citric acid

To make the fizzy sugar, stir together the caster sugar and citric acid until combined. Roll the mamaku cubes in the fizzy sugar just before serving.

SMOKED HARAKEKE CHOCOLATE TRUFFLES

MAKES APPROXIMATELY 50 SMALL TRUFFLES

I love a bit of theatre with my food. At Hiakai, we serve these truffles under a cloche filled with mānuka smoke. The excited expression on diners' faces as their final sweet course is revealed makes every step worth it.

FOR THE CHOCOLATE TERRINE:
125 g unsalted butter
125 g dark chocolate
125 g caster sugar
2 eggs and 1 yolk, lightly beaten

FOR SMOKING:
Mānuka chips
Smoking gun

FOR THE TRUFFLES:
50 g harakeke seeds
200 g dark chocolate

Heat the oven to 180°C. Grease a terrine tin (approx. 20 cm × 10 cm × 7 cm) with baking spray.

Melt the butter and chocolate together in a double-boiler set over low heat. Stir with a rubber spatula until smooth. Remove from the heat.

Whisk together the eggs and sugar to mix, then stir in the melted chocolate until combined. Pour into the prepared tin. Set the tin in a large, deep baking dish. Pour boiling water into the larger dish to a depth of 2 cm. Cover the dish with foil and transfer to the oven. Bake for 30 minutes – the terrine should be just set, like a firm custard, without a crust on the top. Remove the terrine tin from the larger baking dish and allow to cool at room temperature, then cover loosely and chill overnight.

The next day, break the terrine into 2 cm pieces and transfer to a food processor. (Do this in two batches if you have a small machine; don't overload it.)

Set up the smoking gun with mānuka chips and position the smoking tip just above the food processor bowl lid. Start blending the terrine on slow speed. Light the smoking gun and smoke the terrine while the processor is running (don't over-process the terrine or it may split). Taste for smokiness and adjust the flavour if needed.

Transfer the smoked terrine to a piping bag. Pipe 1 cm dots of terrine on a baking paper-lined tray. Freeze overnight.

Heat the oven to 180°C. Put the harakeke seeds between two flat baking sheets (this stops them from flying around the oven) and bake for about 10 minutes. Remove from the oven and allow to cool, then grind into a powder.

While the seeds are baking, roll the piped truffles into small balls and return to the freezer.

Melt the chocolate in a double-boiler set over low heat. Using a skewer, dip each ball into the chocolate and shake off any excess. Roll immediately in the ground harakeke seeds. Leave the coated truffles on a baking-paper-lined tray to set, then store in an airtight container in the fridge.

TARATA MARSHMALLOW

This light and airy marshmallow beautifully harnesses the natural citrus aroma and flavour that tarata has to offer. Serve them torched, or not – they're delicious either way.

FOR THE MARSHMALLOW:

12 g leaf gelatin
50 g egg white
Pinch of table salt
250 g sugar
15 g glucose
40 g water
5 g powdered tarata leaves
2 g ground fennel seed
3 g lemon verbena powder
150 g icing sugar
150 g cornflour

Use baking spray to grease a small baking tray, wiping off any excess. Set aside.

Soak the gelatin leaves in a small bowl of ice-cold water.

Put the egg white and a pinch of table salt in the bowl of a stand mixer fitted with a whisk. Turn the mixer to low speed.

Stir together the sugar, glucose and water in a pot set over medium heat. Cook until the temperature reaches 121°C.

When the sugar is approaching 121°C, increase the mixer speed to medium. Strain the gelatin and put the leaves in a medium pot set over low heat. When they have melted, pour over the sugar syrup and swirl gently to ensure the gelatin is fully dissolved.

Pour this mixture immediately over the egg white in the mixer. Leave the mixer whisking for another 5 minutes, then add in the powdered tarata leaves, fennel and lemon verbena powder. Continue whisking until the mixture is cool.

Sift together the icing sugar and cornflour.

Sprinkle a generous layer over the prepared tray. Pour the cooled marshmallow evenly into the tray and sprinkle more of the icing sugar and cornflour mixture on top. Transfer the tray to the fridge to set for 2 hours. Once set, cut to the desired size (I recommend 2 cm square cubes). Store in an airtight container in the fridge until required.

DRINKS

KAMOKAMO, APPLE, GINGER

2 kamokamo, peeled and deseeded
5 g fresh ginger
50 ml lemon juice
100 ml apple juice
Soda water, to serve

Juice the kamokamo and ginger together. Push the juice through a sieve. Repeat
the sieving process twice more, then add the lemon and apple juice. Push through
a sieve again. Pour into a sterilised bottle and store in the fridge for up to three
days. To serve, mix equal parts soda water and kamokamo, apple and ginger juice.
Decorate with kamokamo crisps (spread leftover kamokamo pulp on a dehydrator
tray and dry for 18 hours at 70°C).

BOYSENBERRY & KAWAKAWA

500 g boysenberries
20 fresh kawakawa leaves
100 ml Simple Syrup (see page 252)
Soda water, to serve

Put the boysenberries, kawakawa leaves and sugar syrup in a blender and purée
until smooth. Push through a sieve and pour the purée into a sterilised bottle.
Store in the fridge. To serve, mix equal parts soda water and boysenberry purée.
Decorate with boysenberry and kawakawa crisps (spread boysenberry pulp on a
dehydrator tray and dry for 18 hours at 70°C).

KAWAKAWA TEA

SERVES 4

6 fresh kawakawa leaves
Fresh ginger or lemon slices, optional

Put the kawakawa leaves in a 500 ml-capacity teapot. Fill with just-boiled water.
Let brew for 8 minutes, then serve. Add fresh ginger or lemon slices if desired.

KOROMIKO TEA

SERVES 4

¼ C fresh koromiko leaves
Fresh ginger or lemon slices, optional

Put the koromiko leaves in a 500 ml-capacity teapot. Fill with just-boiled water. Let
brew for 8 minutes, then serve. Add fresh ginger or lemon slices if desired.

SPICED MANONO TEA

SERVES 4

10 tsp dehydrated manono bark
10 tsp dehydrated tawa bark
2 small star anise
1 tsp dried chamomile flowers
½ cinnamon stick

Grind all the ingredients together in a food processor or with a mortar and pestle.
Store in an airtight container.
To serve, put the spice mixture in a 500 ml-capacity teapot and fill with just-boiled
water. Let brew for 8 minutes, then serve.

MANONO RUM

1 L dark rum
100 g fresh manono bark
100 ml Simple Syrup (see page 252)

Put all the ingredients in a large sterilised jar and stir well. Seal and leave to infuse for three months, at room temperature and in a dark cupboard. After three months, use the rum on its own, in cocktails or in cooking.

MĀNUKA SAUVIGNON

750 ml New Zealand Sauvignon Blanc
40 g fresh mānuka flowers
50 ml Simple Syrup (see page 252)

Put all the ingredients in a large sterilised jar and stir well. Seal and leave to infuse for a month in the fridge. Strain through a coffee filter and transfer to a clean bottle. Store in the fridge until required. Best served chilled.

TARATA SHANDY

FOR THE TARATA SYRUP:
10 dehydrated tarata leaves
100 ml Simple Syrup (see page 252)
250 ml lemon juice

FOR THE SHANDY:
20 ml Tarata Syrup
60 ml zero-alcohol beer
Fresh tarata leaf, to garnish

Mix together the tarata leaves and sugar syrup. Leave to infuse in a jar for a week. Add the lemon juice and mix well. To serve, mix the tarata syrup and beer together. Decorate with tarata leaf.

TARATA SHRUB

RED MATIPO SYRUP

MANONO RUM 31.12.19

KIEKIE

TARATA GIN

PĀTAKA

There are a number of ingredients that we always have on hand in the Hiakai pataka (pantry) to help us create a diverse range of flavours and textures. Many of Aotearoa's native berries and flowers have extremely short seasons, so we are constantly infusing, pickling and dehydrating as much as we can in order to enjoy these ingredients throughout the year. We also use these techniques on plants and kaimoana that are available year-round to extract flavours in new and interesting ways. Over the years, through trial and error, we have developed a selection of staples that feature regularly on our menu. The following pages are some favourites that our pataka will never be without.

CONFIT TĪTĪ

MAKES ONE BIRD
1 whole fresh tītī bird
200 g duck fat
1 bunch of thyme
6 horopito leaves

Put the tītī in a small pot set over medium heat and just cover with cold water. Bring to a simmer, then drain. Transfer the tītī to a dry pot and add the duck fat, thyme, and horopito leaves. Cover and cook over a very low heat to render the fat and flavour from the bird. Strain the fat into a metal bowl and allow to cool. Pull the meat from the bones while the bird is still hot and serve immediately.

INFUSIONS

SIMPLE SYRUP

MAKES 750 ML

500 ml water
500 g white sugar

Put sugar and water in a heavy pot set over medium heat. Bring to a simmer, stirring until the sugar has completely dissolved. Remove from heat and allow to cool, then transfer to a clean bottle or jar. Store in the fridge or in a cool, dark place.

KARAMŪ VINEGAR

MAKES 700 ML

200 g karamū berries, washed and dried
500 ml white wine vinegar

Put the berries in a clean, dry jar or bottle. Pour over the vinegar and seal. Leave at room temperature for at least three weeks to infuse. Store in a cool, dark place.

NASTURTIUM VINEGAR

MAKES 500 ML

100 g nasturtium flowers, brushed to remove dirt
50 g nasturtium leaves, washed and dried
500 ml Chardonnay vinegar

Put the flowers and leaves in a clean glass jar and pour over the vinegar. Cover tightly and leave to infuse for at least a week at room temperature. Store in a cool, dark place.

HARAKEKE BLOSSOM SYRUP

MAKES 500 ML

150 g harakeke blossoms
500 ml Simple Syrup

Put the blossoms in a glass jar and pour over the syrup. Cover tightly and leave to infuse for at least a month at room temperature. Store in a cool, dark place.

KIEKIE GIN

MAKES 650 ML

3 kiekie flowers (petals and buds), washed and dried
150 ml Simple Syrup
500 ml neutral-flavoured gin

Put all ingredients in a glass jar and stir to combine. Cover tightly and leave to infuse for at least 10 days at room temperature. Store in a cool, dark place.

RED MATIPO SYRUP

MAKES 600 ML

20 g red matipo leaves, dried
10 g fresh tarata leaves
600 ml Simple Syrup

Put all ingredients in a glass jar. Cover tightly and leave to infuse for at least 10 days at room temperature. Store in a cool, dark place.

RED MATIPO SYRUP

TARATA GIN

MAKES 700 ML

50 g tarata flowers
200 ml Simple Syrup
500 ml neutral-flavoured gin

Put the flowers, syrup and gin in a glass jar and stir to combine. Cover tightly and leave to infuse for at least a month at room temperature. Store in a cool, dark place.

TARATA SHRUB

MAKES 800 ML

50 g tarata flowers
50 ml Chardonnay vinegar
750 ml cider vinegar

Put the flowers and vinegars in a glass jar. Cover tightly and leave to infuse for at least a month at room temperature. Store in a cool, dark place.

PINE OIL

MAKES 1 L

1 bunch fresh green pine needles
1 L grapeseed or olive oil

Put the pine needles in a bottle and fill with the oil. Seal and leave in a Roner (a thermostat-controlled water bath) to infuse for 4 hours at 60°C. Cool and store at room temperature.

RED MATIPO

MANONO BARK

KARAMU

BULL KELP

KARENGO

KIO KIO

PIKOPIKO

TI KOUKA HEARTS

HOROPITO

PICKLED

SWEET PICKLE BASE

MAKES 930 ML

600 ml white wine vinegar
300 g caster sugar
30 g table salt

Put all the ingredients in a heavy pot set over medium heat. Bring to a simmer, stirring until the sugar and salt have completely dissolved. Remove from heat and allow to cool, then transfer to a clean bottle or jar. Store in a cool, dark place.

BRINE PICKLE BASE

MAKES 675 ML

300 ml white wine vinegar
300 ml water
60 g caster sugar
15 g table salt

Put all the ingredients in a heavy pot set over medium heat. Bring to a simmer, stirring until the sugar and salt have completely dissolved. Remove from heat and allow to cool, then transfer to a clean bottle or jar. Store in a cool, dark place.

PICKLED PIKOPIKO

MAKES 150 G

150 g pikopiko shoots, washed and dried
150 ml Brine Pickle Base

Put the pikopiko shoots in a small, sterilised preserving jar. Cover with the brine and seal tightly.

Preserve in a water bath – put the jar in a small pot and cover with cold water. Cover with a lid and bring to a gentle boil. Boil for 8 minutes, then remove from the water bath and allow to cool. Store in a cool, dark place.

PICKLED SUPPLEJACK TIPS

MAKES 150 G

150 g supplejack tips, washed and dried
150 ml Brine Pickle Base

Put the supplejack in a small, sterilised preserving jar. Cover with the brine and seal tightly.

Preserve in a water bath – put the jar in a small pot and cover with cold water. Cover with a lid and bring to a gentle boil. Boil for 8 minutes, then remove from the water bath and allow to cool. Store in a cool, dark place.

SWEET PICKLED PŪHĀ

MAKES 1 L

1 bunch pūhā, washed well and squeezed to remove any excess water
150–200 ml Sweet Pickle Base

Put the pūhā in a sterilised preserving jar. Cover with the Sweet Pickle Base and seal tightly.

Preserve in a water bath – put the jar in a small pot and cover with cold water. Cover with a lid and bring to a gentle boil. Boil for 15 minutes, then remove from the water bath and allow to cool. Store at room temperature.

SWEET PICKLED TĪ KŌUKA HEARTS

MAKES 150 G

150 g tī kōuka hearts, washed and dried
150 ml Sweet Pickle Base

Put the tī kōuka hearts in a small sterilised preserving jar. Cover with the Sweet Pickle Base and seal tightly.

Preserve in a water bath – put the jar in a small pot and cover with cold water. Cover with a lid and bring to a gentle boil. Boil for 20 minutes, then remove from the water bath and allow to cool. Store at room temperature.

DRIED

HARAKEKE SEEDS

Pick only the dry, black pods from the harakeke. Break them open over a bowl to collect the seeds. Spread the seeds over a baking-paper-lined dehydrator tray and dry for 2 hours at 60°C. Transfer to an airtight container and store at room temperature.

HOROPITO LEAVES

Clean the leaves under running water and dry thoroughly with a cloth. Spread the leaves between two oven grill racks laid on top of each other. Dry in the sun or in a well-ventilated room. Store dried leaves in an airtight container at room temperature.

KARENGO

Clean the karengo under running water and dry thoroughly with a cloth. Spread out on a dehydrator tray, making sure it doesn't overlap. Dry for 5 hours at 65°C. Transfer to an airtight container and store at room temperature.

KAWAKAWA BERRIES

Arrange washed and dried berries on a dehydrator tray. Dry for 10 hours at 70°C. Transfer to an airtight container and store at room temperature.

KAWAKAWA LEAVES

Arrange washed and dried leaves on a dehydrator tray, making sure they don't overlap. Dry for 4 hours at 60°C. Transfer to an airtight container and store at room temperature.

KIOKIO SHOOTS

Arrange washed and dried shoots on a dehydrator tray, making sure they don't overlap. Dry for 5 hours at 65°C. Transfer to an airtight container and store at room temperature.

MANONO BARK

Scrub any lichen off the bark and arrange the bark on a dehydrator tray, making sure it doesn't overlap. Don't overload the tray. Dry for 8–12 hours at 65°C (the time will depend on the bark's thickness). Transfer to an airtight container and store at room temperature.

MANONO LEAVES

Clean the leaves under running water and dry thoroughly with a cloth. Tie leaves with butcher's twine and hang in a cellar or well-ventilated room. Store dried leaves in an airtight container at room temperature.

MŌKEHU SHOOTS

Arrange washed and dried shoots on a dehydrator tray, making sure they don't overlap. Dry for 5 hours at 65°C. Transfer to an airtight container and store at room temperature.

MUSSEL OR PIPI POWDER

Set a heavy saucepan over medium heat and add 500 g shellfish. Cover and cook until all the shells have opened (discard any that don't open). Allow to cool. Strain the juices and save for another use. Remove and discard the shells. Arrange the cooked shellfish on a dehydrator tray (line it with baking paper if the gaps are too big). Dry for 12 hours at 70°C. Once fully dried, grind to a powder with a spice grinder. Transfer to an airtight container and store at room temperature.

GLOSSARY OF KEY MĀORI TERMS

ATUA
God, deity or supernatural
being.

HĀNGI
Cooking, or food cooked,
in an underground earth
oven. For early Māori this
was everyday practice;
today a hāngi is a major
event.

HAPŪ
Subtribe, kinship group,
clan.

HUE
A gourd plant mainly
grown for use as food or
water containers.

HUI
A meeting or gathering.

KĀURU
Food produced from tī
kouka, the cabbage tree.

KIORE HUAHUA
Preserved rat, a delicacy
saved for visitors.

KŌ
Wooden digging sticks
used for harvesting crops,
such as aruhe.

KŌRITO
Edible young leaf shoots of
plants, such as tī kouka.

MAHINGA KAI
Food-gathering places,
the food collected at these
places, and the tikanga
surrounding this gathering.

MANAAKITANGA
Hospitality, including the
care of manuhiri.

MANUHIRI
Visitors or guests.

MĀRA
A food garden or
cultivation.

MĀTAURANGA MĀORI
Knowledge and
understanding of the Māori
world (te ao Māori).

PĀTAKA
A storehouse or pantry.

RĀHUI
A ritual prohibition set for
a period of time.

ROHE
A boundary or area of
land.

RONGOĀ MĀORI
Māori medicine, including
natural and traditional
treatments.

ROUROU
A small woven basket used
for cooking and serving
food. Rourou are also a
symbol of manaakitanga.

TAONGA
Anything considered
precious or of value,
whether personal, social or
cultural.

TIKANGA
Correct protocol and
learned value systems for
different contexts.

WAUWAU
A paddle-shaped wooden
digging tool.

WHAKAPAPA
Ancestry, lineage,
bloodline.

WHĀNAU
Family group or extended
family. Can also apply to a
group of friends or people
without kinship ties.

ACKNOWLEDGEMENTS

First and foremost, I'd like to thank my parents, Serena and Siuai, who have been my biggest supporters and instrumental to Hiakai's success.

Much love to my four siblings Estelle, Luke, Elijah and Shannah. No matter what I need a hand with, be it digging a hāngi pit or last minute painting, I can count on you to be there.

I also need to mention two very important women in my life, Nanny Jenny and Nanny Tepora.

You both represent the true strength of wāhine and this has had a profound impact on my life and career.

Thank you to Jeremy Sherlock, your patience and support during the writing of this book can't be overstated. Tracy Berno and Lucy Corry, thank you for walking alongside me. Thank you to Grace Thomas for all of the hard work.

Manja Wachsmuth and Amber-Jayne Bain, thank you for capturing my food and journey so beautifully.

A big shout-out to the entire team at Hiakai, past and present. Many wonderful people have contributed to this body of work and I feel immense gratitude.

Last but not least, I'd like to thank my partner Katie Monteith who kept me fed and motivated to the very end.

Monique Fiso
September 2020

To the many others who contributed to the making of the book – Hannah Braithwaite, Thea Ceramics, Fiona Mackay, Homeground NZ, Hayley Bridgeford, Mammoth Glass Studio, Easterbrook Farms, Old School Reserve Teaching Gardens, Ambury Farm, Fish & Game New Zealand – thank you.

Manja Wachsmuth

Thank you to two strong and clever women – Monique and Manja. You both took a chance on me in friendship and creative endeavour, and you are precious to me. Thank you to Jonathan, my anchor, and to Max, for the fun on set.

Amber-Jayne Bain

PROPS + INGREDIENTS

Thea Ceramics,
thea-ceramics.com, @thea_ceramics
Hayley Bridgford,
@hayleybridgfordceramics
Fiona Mackay,
fionamackayceramics.co.nz,
@fionamackayceramics
Homeground NZ,
homeground.nz, @homegroundnz
Monmouth Glass Studio,
monmouthglassstudio.com,
@monmouthglassstudio
Old School Reserve Teaching
Gardens, Mangere, Yvonne Thomas:
yvonnethomas1946@gmail.com
Ambury Farm, Janine Nillesen:
janine.nillesen@aucklandcouncil.govt.nz

SOURCES

Beaton, S. (2008). 'A contemporary Māori culinary tradition – does it exist?: An analysis of Māori cuisine'. Unpublished MA thesis. Dunedin: University of Otago.

Best, E. (2004). *The Maori as he was: A brief account of Maori life as it was in pre-European days.* Wellington: New Zealand Electronic Text Collection.

—— (2005). *Fishing methods and devices of the Māori.* Wellington: Te Papa Press.

—— (2005). *Forest lore of the Māori: with methods of snaring, trapping, and preserving birds and rats, uses of berries, roots, fern-root, and forest products, with mythological notes on origins, karakia used, etc.* Wellington: Te Papa Press.

—— (2005). *Māori agriculture. Cultivated food-plants of the Māori and native methods of agriculture.* Wellington: Te Papa Press.

—— (2005). *Māori storehouses and kindred structures.* Wellington: Te Papa Press.

Burtenshaw, M. (2009). 'A guide to growing pre-European Māori kūmara in the traditional manner'. Lower Hutt: The Open Polytechnic of New Zealand.

Christchurch City Libraries (2018). 'Tī Kōuka – The Cabbage Tree'. https://my.christchurchcitylibraries.com/ti-kouka-the-cabbage-tree.

Colenso, W. (2001). *On the vegetable food of the ancient New Zealanders before Cook's visit.* Christchurch: KiwiPublishers.

Cowan, J. (2007). *The Māori: yesterday and to-day.* Wellington:

New Zealand Electronic Text Collection.

Crowe, A. (2004). *A Field Guide to the Native Edible Plants of New Zealand.* Auckland: Penguin.

Dacker, B. (1990). *The people of the place: mahika kai.* Wellington: New Zealand 1990 Commission.

de la Cerda, R. E. (2015). 'Traditional knowledge systems and crops: Case studies on the introduction of kūmara (Ipomoea batatas) and taewa Māori (Solanum tuberosum) to Aotearoa/New Zealand.' Unpublished Master of AgriScience thesis. Palmerston North: Massey University.

Fuller, J. D. (1978). *Maori Food and Cookery.* Wellington: Reed.

Furey, L. (2006). 'Maori gardening: An archaeological perspective'. Wellington: Department of Conservation.

Hamilton, A. (1908). 'Fishing and sea-foods of the ancient Maori', *Bulletin,* no. 2, Dominion Museum. Wellington: Government Printer.

Harmsworth, G. R. & Awatere, S. (2013). 'Indigenous Māori knowledge and perspectives of ecosystems'. In Dymond, J. R. (ed.), *Ecosystem services in New Zealand – conditions and trends.* Lincoln: Manaaki Whenua Press.

Harris, P., Matamua, R., Smith, T., Kerr, H. & Waaka, T. (2013). 'A review of Māori astronomy in Aotearoa–New Zealand.' In *Journal of Astronomical History and Heritage,* 16(3).

Henare, M. 'Te mahi kai – food production economics – Adapting to New Zealand'. Te Ara – the

Encyclopedia of New Zealand. http://www.TeAra.govt.nz/en/te-mahi-kai-food-production-economics/page-2

Hiroa, T. (2009). *The Coming of the Maori.* Wellington: New Zealand Electronic Text Collection.

Hutchings, J. (2015). *Te Mahi Māra Hua Parakore: A Māori food sovereignty handbook.* Ōtaki: Te Tākupu, Te Wānanga o Raukawa.

Landcare Research Manaaki Whenua (2018). 'Ngā Tipu Whakaoranga: Māori plant use.' Accessible at: https://maoriplantuse.landcareresearch.co.nz/WebForms/default.aspx

Langlands, P. (2014). *New Zealand Seaweed Foraging Guide.* Christchurch: Wild Capture.

Leach, H. (1984). *1,000 Years of Gardening in New Zealand.* Wellington: Reed.

—— (2010). 'Maori cookery before Cook.' In Leach, H. (ed.), *From Kai to Kiwi Kitchen: New Zealand Culinary Traditions.* Dunedin: Otago University Press.

Ministry of Environment (2010). *Resource Management Act 1991: Māori Values Supplement.* Publication reference: ME 679. Wellington: Ministry of the Environment.

Moon, P. (2005). *A Tohunga's Natural World: Plants, gardening and food.* Auckland: David Ling Publishing.

Moorfield, J. C. (2003–20). 'Te Aka Online Māori Dictionary.' Accessible at: https://maoridictionary.co.nz

Murton, B. (2000). 'Australia and New Zealand.' In Kiple, K. F. & Ornelas, K.C. (eds), *The Cambridge World History of Food* (vol. 2). Cambridge, UK: Cambridge University Press.

'New Zealand Birds Online: The digital encyclopaedia of New Zealand birds'. http://nzbirdsonline.org.nz

Orbell, M. (1996). *The Natural World of the Maori*. Auckland: David Bateman.

Overbeek, A. (nd). *Ahurea i roto i kai: maori culture through cuisine*. https://issuu.com/ashley_leah/docs/maori_food_book_final_draft

Paulin, C. D. (2007). 'Perspectives of Māori fishing history and techniques: Ngā āhua me ngā pūrākau me ngā hangarau ika o te Māori'. In *Tuhinga* 18: Records of the Museum of New Zealand Te Papa Tongarewa.

Phillipps, W. J. (1952). *Maori houses and food stores*. Wellington: Government Printer.

Phillipps, W. J.; rev. by Huria, J. (2008). *Māori Life and Custom*. Auckland: Raupō.

Phillips, C., Jackson, A-M. & Hakopa, H. (2016). 'Creation Narratives of Mahinga Kai: Māori customary food-gathering sites and practices'. In *MAI Journal*, 5(1).

Richardson, R. (2017). '3 feet under: Is the traditional hāngī in danger of a cultural disappearance?' Unpublished Master of Gastronomy thesis. Auckland: Auckland University of Technology.

Riley, M. (1998). *Maori Vegetable Cooking: Traditional and Modern Methods*. Paraparaumu: Viking Sevenseas.

Roberts, M. (2013). 'Ways of Seeing: Whakapapa'. In *Sites: A Journal of Social Anthropology and Cultural Studies*, 10(1).

Roberts, M., Weko, F., & Clarke, L. (2006). 'Maramataka: The Maori Moon Calendar'. Lincoln: Lincoln University, Agribusiness and Economics Research Unit.

Roskruge, N. (2015). *Tahua-roa: Food for your visitors – Karore: Māori green vegetables, their history and tips on their use*. Palmerston North: Institute of Natural Resources, Massey University.

—— (2014). *Rauwaru: The proverbial garden – Ngā-weri: Māori root vegetables their history and tips on their use*. Palmerston North: Institute of Natural Resources, Massey University.

Ross, J. (2005). *Technology of the Māori: A study of food from moa hunter to pre-European settlement*. New Plymouth: Curriculum Concepts.

Rout, E. (1926). *Native diet: with numerous practical recipes*. London: Heinemann.

Royal, T. A. C. (ed.) (2003). *The Woven Universe: Selected writings of Rev. Māori Marsden*. Ōtaki: The Estate of Rev. Māori Marsden.

Solomon, R. (2014). *An overview of sensitive areas in Kaikoura in response to an application for a Global Archaeological Authority by Chorus Ltd*. Te Runanga o Kaikoura for New Zealand Heritage Properties Ltd.

Stevens, M. (2014). 'Pōhā: A clever way of storing food'. In *School Journal*, Level 2, September 2014. Wellington: Ministry of Education.

Te Ao Hou: The New World (1962). 'The Old Maori Water Bottles'. In *Te Ao Hou: The New World*, 39.

Te Ara Encyclopedia of New Zealand (2010). *Te Taiao: Māori and the Natural World*. Auckland: David Bateman.

Te Toa Takitini (1924). 'Manaakitanga'. In *Te Toa Takitini*, 85.

Tregear, E. (2005). *The Māori Race*. Wellington: New Zealand Electronic Text Collection.

Walker, R. (2004). *Ka Whawhai Tonu Matou: Struggle Without End*. Auckland: Penguin.

Walsh, P. (1902). *The Cultivation and Treatment of the Kumara by the Primitive Maoris*. Transactions and Proceeding of the Royal Society of New Zealand, 1868–1961. Accessible at: http://rsnz.natlib.govt.nz/volume/rsnz_35/rsnz_35_00_000510.html

INDEX